'We live in interesting and complex times. Mod⸱ and freedom to shape our destiny in many, often church is only one place where the shape of human experience is opened up and attended to in our struggle to flourish. This context provides us an opportunity to reimagine how theology and its practice might contribute to well-being. *Performing Pastoral Care* is a serious and substantial contribution to our understanding of this practice as it calls us all to rediscover our pastoral heart with imagination and creativity. Interdisciplinary in its focus, music and theology both blend and dialogue to provide a stimulating, intelligent and well-organised narrative. The reader is asked to look outwards through a number of lenses and using a variety of methods to engage with the paradoxes and ambiguities of human experience. It succeeds in providing a significant contribution to the literature around music and pastoral theology, and its carefully organised chapters offer practical tools for the resourcing of the shapes of pastoral activity and performance. I hope that it will be widely used as part of the ongoing conversation about what might need to be transformed in and through us as we seek to reach out and serve our world and its peoples. I shall be adding it to core reading lists for my students.'

— *The Revd Dr James Woodward,*
Principal of Sarum College

'A haunting book. Clifton-Smith tenderly unsettles the church's modernist notions of mission with his musical and pastoral explorations of life in all its rawness. His use of musical form as a template for chaplaincy is lodged in my soul. I look forward to many variations and performances of this rich theme as his work reaches a wide, and appreciative, audience.'

— *The Revd Canon Dr Margaret Whipp, Lead*
Chaplain, Oxford University Hospitals

'Gregory Clifton-Smith's book is a rare and exceptional contribution to the field of pastoral theology – imaginative, inspired, creative and clever. The arena of pastoral theology is normally dominated by books that focus on reflection, applications or techniques, so it is refreshing to find a profound volume such as *Performing Pastoral Care*, offering such an original insight into how pastoral care can be both imagined and practised. Gregory Clifton-Smith's book is both wise and winsome, and will repay careful reading for all those engaged in mission and ministry.'

— *The Very Revd Prof. Martyn Percy, Dean,*
Christ Church, Oxford

PERFORMING PASTORAL CARE

Music as a Framework for
Exploring Pastoral Care

Gregory Clifton-Smith

Foreword by Dr June Boyce-Tillman

Jessica Kingsley *Publishers*
London and Philadelphia

Copyright acknowledgements are listed at the bottom of page 13.

Disclaimer: Every effort has been made to trace copyright holders and to obtain their permission for the use of copyright material. The author and the publisher apologize for any omissions and would be grateful if notified of any acknowledgements that should be incorporated in future reprints or editions of this book.

First published in 2016
by Jessica Kingsley Publishers
73 Collier Street
London N1 9BE, UK
and
400 Market Street, Suite 400
Philadelphia, PA 19106, USA

www.jkp.com

Copyright © Gregory Clifton-Smith 2016
Foreword copyright © June Boyce-Tillman 2016

Printed digitally since 2016

Library of Congress Cataloging in Publication Data
Names: Clifton-Smith, Gregory, author.
Title: Performing pastoral care : music as a framework for exploring pastoral
  care / Gregory Clifton-Smith ; foreword by Dr June Boyce-Tillman.
Description: Philadelphia : Jessica Kingsley Publishers, 2016. | Includes
  bibliographical references and index.
Identifiers: LCCN 2016014034 | ISBN 9781785920363 (alk. paper)
Subjects: LCSH: Pastoral care. | Music--Religious aspects--Christianity.
Classification: LCC BV4011.3 .C55 2016 | DDC 253--dc23
LC record available at http://lccn.loc.gov/2016014034

British Library Cataloguing in Publication Data
A CIP catalogue record for this book is available from the British Library

ISBN 978 1 78592 036 3
eISBN 978 1 78450 287 4

In memory of, and in grateful thanks to, my parents, Monica Frances Redgrave and Peter James Smith, to whom I owe so much.

CONTENTS

FOREWORD

This is an exciting book from a person dedicated to interdisciplinary enquiry into the two fields of his vocation – music and chaplaincy. By using music as a metaphor, the author manages to throw new light on to the complex area of pastoral care – insights that would not have been revealed if he had stayed within the discipline of pastoral theology. In this use of music, he follows in the footsteps of theologians such as the medieval abbess Hildegard of Bingen, who saw us as being played like a harp in God's hands. He claims that each generation needs to generate its own metaphors from their lived experience. He has certainly done that, using contemporary classical compositions. His grasp of both subjects – music and theology – makes this an enlightening and challenging text; but it is also very readable. He uses a crystallizing methodology which sees truth as a crystal to be viewed through different lenses. We have journal entries, musical examples, poetry from St John of the Cross and also the author's own creative work rubbing shoulders with one another in the text and revealing different aspects of pastoral care.

The complex and paradoxical nature of meaning in music enables the expression of the uncertainties within both music and pastoral theology – the interweaving of contradictory strands – private/public, justice/wellbeing, and finally and importantly the relationship between mission and pastoral care. The stress in the hierarchy of the Anglican Church on parish ministry has led the authorities regularly to ignore and marginalize chaplaincy; yet chaplains (like self-supporting priests) are already out there in the wider world and do not need to work out how to get out of the world of the Church; they are there already. In my training as a non-stipendiary priest, I was deeply disappointed about how much of the course concentrated on parish ministry – for which, as a university professor, I had limited time. There was no attention to paid to how my priesthood might be exercised in my everyday working life, where I was working alongside a variety of people of many faith traditions and none – people who regularly ask questions about faith and meaning.

Chaplaincy is a rich and fertile field for a renewed theology of mission. As the author draws out from his own experience, colonial models of mission are inappropriate in this context. I love how the author gets to the central point in his last chapter, defining the chaplain's ministry as incarnating God's love in the world. This links with Pope John Paul II's description of the artist's vocation to produce epiphanies of beauty. The author sees how pastoral care sits uneasily with managerial models of church leadership. The case studies allow us to see the complexity of secular contexts and the way that individuals are searching to build and construct meaning in situations of distress and loss.

I am particularly pleased to see liturgy explored here, which he describes as a holding form (like the way in which people use music in everyday life) in the context of a society/Church that can see ritual as dead. I felt when priests started to train as psychotherapists they often forgot that they were priests. The author pulls them back to their priestly calling, one of the tools of which is liturgy and prayer. He uses music to clarify the strands in the pastoral relationship. He uses the metaphor of harmony with no melody to describe the counselling model – depth but no breadth – whereas the mission managerial leadership is likened to a melody with no harmony – breadth with no depth. He goes on to see that attentive pastoral care can be likened to harmony and melody in equal measure, with both depth and breadth in equal balance. It is a fine metaphor.

I also love how the author's own musical composition is a theological statement. *Collage* is able to encompass the paradox of knowing mixed with the not-knowing which is a part of any faith journey. Here again he resembles Hildegard, who expressed her Virtue theology most clearly in her music theatre piece, *Ordo Virtutum, The Play of the Powers*. He develops a theology of music which, as a composer, I find immensely exciting – dealing so sensitively with Britten, Tippett and Messiaen as well as my own and his own work. Drawing on Lucy Winkett, he sees music as expressing our inner wounding, in the same way as the stories of the people he cares for. He then draws on the image that I have used, of our inner musician as the divine healer within us; this is a similar image to the awakening of the God within the subjects of his own pastoral care. He draws out how woundedness is reflected in Tippett's theme of the scapegoat and the tritone interval in Messiaen's *Quartet for the End of Time* and Britten's *War Requiem*, where it remains the unresolved unity of the work right to the end, just like the some of the case study stories. He reads my own *Space for Peace* well, seeing its transient, changing nature and the juxtaposition of diversity and unity in the struggle for reconciliation. Again this parallels the inner struggles of many of the case studies.

In putting together a whole range of literatures and analysing their similarities and differences, he goes a long way towards seeing how religious narratives might function in a post-secular society. Contemporary society is not like the secularizing Western world that I have lived through; it is again desirous of some sense of the beyond and the holy, while often being suspicious of rooting it in mainstream traditions. The author shows how a Christian priest can be rooted in a tradition and yet able to reach out to a world where a variety of meaning-making systems compete for supremacy. Like the Celtic story of St Brendan sailing around these islands on his pilgrimage in his little boat, the author skilfully navigates a way through contemporary life in hospitals, by drawing and contemplating effectively on lived experience. Here he questions the often expressed position of bringing God into a situation and defines his ministry as seeing where God is already at work in a world that is in its very nature infused with the Divine. This contrasts strongly with the colonial version of the missionary enterprises of the past. His ministry includes careful listening, not only to the lamenting, but also to the righteous anger over the injustice built into institutions like the health service which he links with divine anger against injustice.

I feel privileged to have been able to read this book. It has enriched my thinking, and I am sure others will be inspired and informed by it.

The Revd Dr June Boyce-Tillman MBE FRSA FHEA,
Professor of Applied Music and Artistic Convenor for the
Centre for the Arts as Wellbeing, University of Winchester,
Extraordinary Professor at North-West University, South Africa

MUSICAL QUOTATIONS

3.1 *A Child of Our Time* – Extract from second Spiritual (Nobody knows)

3.2 *A Child of Our Time* – Extract from final Spiritual (Deep river)

3.3 *Quatuor pour la fin du temps* – (a) Extract from 'Danse de la fureur'

3.4 *Quatuor pour la fin du temps* – (b) Extract from 'Danse de la fureur'

3.5 *War Requiem* – Extract from 'Requiem Aeternam'

3.6 *War Requiem* – Extract from 'Agnus Dei'

3.7 *War Requiem* – Extract from 'Dies Irae'

3.8 *Collage* – (a) Extract from the love theme

3.9 *Collage* – (b) Extract from atonal material

3.10 *Collage* – (c) Extract from repeated rhythmic pattern

3.11 *Space for Peace* – Traditional chant (Shalom salaam…)

I am grateful to the following publishers for allowing me to include musical examples for which they hold the copyright:

ACKNOWLEDGEMENTS

In the production of this book, I am indebted to the following:

Professor Elaine Graham, who encouraged me to begin the doctoral programme out of which this book sprang; the Revd Prebendary Dr Peter Speck, who enabled me to reflect theologically upon clinical pastoral encounters; Dr Natalie Watson, who allowed me to think that the writing of this book might be possible; the Dean and Chapter of Winchester Cathedral for giving me the time to bring the first draft of this book into being; Anne Lewin for her diligent proofreading before the final draft of this book was submitted for publication; Richard Pratt for facilitating the inclusion of the musical examples; the Revd Professor June Boyce-Tillman for kindly agreeing to write the Foreword; and finally to my wife, Robbie, for her patient support and encouragement.

INTRODUCTION

Central to both the practice of pastoral care and the execution of music making is the activity of listening. Can the latter inform the former so that those involved in pastoral care can be challenged to listen in a new way? It is in order to test this idea that this book will attempt to look at pastoral care through the prism of classical music. My hope is that it will present pastoral care in a new way, concentrating on its *formative* and *participatory* functions. The justification of this approach is rooted in an understanding of practical theology (of which pastoral care may be understood to form a part) defined by Pattison and Lynch (2005, pp.410–11), which values 'an interdisciplinary approach' in bringing about 'theoretical and practical transformation' in this field. The term 'collage' (although originating in the visual arts, like impressionism, but equally applicable in the world of music) is usually used to describe a creative process in which various, often contrasting, materials are juxtaposed to form a new work of art. It thus lends itself well to describing, from a musical perspective, Pattison and Lynch's idea of setting received tradition alongside practical experience, which, in turn, advocates a model of theology in which 'critical dialogue' and 'theological reflection' generate 'new insights' (pp.412, 415–18). This book will look at how both practical theology and classical music share interactions between a *received tradition* and a *lived contemporary experience*, and then explore how musical form can inform the understanding, and musical performance inform the practice, of pastoral care. It will conclude by exploring how pastoral care can be validated in an increasingly mission-focused environment. Whilst telling of certainties that are imported from without a situation rather than listening to uncertainties that are discovered within a situation may at first glance appear to have the upper hand here, I will argue that rather than being contradictory elements within ministry, pastoral care and mission offer a sense of complementarity, the one in fact being an outworking of the other.

Because my own pastoral experience has been principally within the area of healthcare chaplaincy, the *received tradition* and *lived contemporary experience* I shall focus on will also be taken from this, or related, areas of pastoral care. The classical musical compositions I focus on are those born out of the trauma of war and social fragmentation. Those aspects of musical form I refer to will be those used in the canon from 1600 to the present day. Those aspects of musical performance I draw on are be rooted in those who initiate and those who receive musical sound. By combining this with the hermeneutic and pastoral cycles, I shall propose a performative meaning-making cycle as a model for pastoral care. Through the musical analogy of pastoral care being harmonically rooted, and evangelical zeal being melodically driven, I shall suggest that an holistic understanding of both, in vibrant relationship one with the other, is essential if the Church's ministerial performance is to have any chance of being fit for purpose and of standing the test of time.

1

LISTENING TO THE VOICE OF HISTORICAL EXPERIENCE

Surviving the Darkness of Imprisonment

This chapter begins the process of engaging in 'critical dialogue between theological norms and contemporary experience' (Pattison and Lynch 2005, pp.410–11) and explores whether this position can be supported by examples taken from an historical perspective. This chapter will use examples from literal and metaphorical imprisonment by way of illuminating the restrictions patients can feel are placed upon them when their freedom of movement and/or daily routine is changed by being hospitalized or by having to process a serious illness or disability. The areas I shall explore will include imprisonment as a result of armed conflict, ethnic persecution and abuse. The conversation partners I shall engage with are the palliative care consultant Sheila Cassidy, the sixteenth-century Carmelite monk St John of the Cross, the mid-twentieth-century Lutheran pastor Dietrich Bonhoeffer, the contemporary theologians Miroslav Volf and Alistair McFadyen, and the psychologist Viktor Frankl, who also lived and worked in the middle of the last century. For those people of faith who find themselves thrust into suffering, in the hope of surviving such difficult dark experiences, there is the parallel problem of sensing or not sensing the presence or absence of God.

At the end of her book *Sharing the Darkness*, in the process of herself engaging in 'critical dialogue between theological norms and contemporary experience' (see above), Sheila Cassidy (b. 1937) asks the question 'How can we believe in a God who allows suffering?' She offers four possible suggestions:

1. There is no God and things just happen in a random way.

2. God is unable to control the elements in the world that he has created.

3. God can control them but chooses not to.

4. God is somehow involved in every person's life and actually arranges that some people suffer more than others, because it is part of his great cosmic plan.

(Cassidy 1988, pp.156–7)

It is clear that Cassidy favours the fourth point. I wonder whether there is a fifth point to be added to Cassidy's list:

5. Suffering simply is. It exists, because it is an integral part of the world as it has been created.

In a world, indeed in a universe, which is always changing, there will always be growth and decay just as there will always be birth and death. To eliminate suffering would result in changing the universe as we presently perceive it – indeed, to such an extent that we may not be present to perceive it at all! Cassidy is a palliative care consultant and a former political prisoner, who suffered torture whilst she was incarcerated (arrested by members of the Pinochet regime in Chile for tending to a wounded person perceived by them as the enemy). What concerns her, as it will concern everyone, with a faith or not, working in healthcare, is the sheer degree of suffering that some patients find themselves experiencing, and our apparent inability to mitigate it in any meaningful way. For Cassidy, as for anybody who has undergone any kind of suffering in their own life, ministering to the sick puts each of us in touch once again with our own brokenness and vulnerability.

PATIENT EXPERIENCE

At the bedside, patients frequently ask, 'What have I done to deserve this? Why is God punishing me in this way? Why won't God heal me? Why do bad things happen to good people?' These theological questions demand a better response from the chaplain than 'I don't know'. Otherwise, the chaplain can appear as impotent or irrelevant as the God he/she purports to represent. But giving patients answers born out of too much certainty can be equally unhelpful. In asking the question, there is an assumption by the patient that there is an answer. If this yearning to know 'why' is not taken seriously, the anger a patient feels towards God can be projected on to the chaplain. In seeking to respond to the patient's enquiry, there needs to be a gentle probing into the nature of the God in which they believe, a matter made all the more difficult if the patient has very little understanding of God which they feel able to share with others in the first place. As with any journey, the only place to begin is where you actually are and not where you would like to be. If the patient knows nothing of a loving God, but has experienced the giving and receiving of love in relationship, recognizing God in that love is a necessary first step. If the patient views God as being involved in and affected by their suffering, as supporting them and holding their hand, perhaps assisted by the chaplain acting *in loco Dei*, who is actually supporting them and holding their hand, they may well discover, in the middle of their suffering, a sense of God's presence rather than being convinced of his absence. Patients seem to be in no danger of muddling up God with his representative. In talking specifically of the dying patient, Cassidy says, the patients 'know we are not God... All they ask is that we do not desert them' (1988, p.64).

Darkness

Perhaps the best exponent of discovering, in the midst of suffering, a sense of God's presence rather than being convinced of his absence, is St John of the Cross (1542–1591), imprisoned in 1577 by anti-reformist Carmelites, who saw John as epitomizing all those who sought to reform the religious status quo. Whilst he was still in prison in Toledo, John wrote an initial eight-stanza poem (the 40 lines of the poem gives a Lenten feel to the whole venture), which began to explore how humankind might aspire to union with God, how humankind might move from meditation towards contemplation (St John of the Cross 2003, pp.1–2, 25; Book 1, Ch. 9, 9; see also Appendix 1). He further reflected on these in two subsequent works: *The Ascent of Mount Carmel*, in which he comments on the active role of humankind in this process; and *The Dark Night of the Soul* on the passive role of God. Whilst John writes in a time when a Christian faith could be assumed, his relevance to subsequent generations, including our own, is his continual wrestling to find an authentic and honest way to speak about his experience of God at work, even when God appears to be absent.

It is clear from his poem, and his reflections upon it, that John sees darkness not as a time to be feared, but as a time when God makes space in our lives to receive him. Darkness is an essential prerequisite for this new life to take root. His experience of God in the midst of his imprisonment was that of darkness, in which 'the only alternatives are a Spirit who fills, or chaos' (Matthew 1995, p.10). In the middle of the darkness, John senses 'a certain companionship and strength which bears it company and so greatly strengthens it' (St John of the Cross 2003, p.70; Book 2, Ch. 11, 7). But before one can experience this companionship, there must be space made for God to come into our lives. This space can be experienced as emptiness. But Matthew, a commentator on his work, points out that for John, 'Absence of insight or feeling – even if it leaves the person "in dryness, in darkness, feeling abandoned" – does not certify that God is any further away' (Canticle 2nd redaction 1.4, cited in Matthew 1995, p.32). Or, put another way, 'If God is beyond us, his approach is also liable to leave us feeling out of our depth' (Matthew 1995, p.56). Furthermore, it is God himself that 'undertakes to create that space... He calls it "night"' (Matthew 1995, p.51).

Darkness would seem to be used by John as a very rich metaphor, capable of a variety of meanings. Darkness can feel restrictive and prison-like. But, paradoxically, it can also be regarded as bringing with it a clarity of vision, free from the distractions of the light-polluting day. God can appear dark because we simply cannot compute his brightness, 'our field of vision' being 'too narrow' (Matthew 1995, p.104). Matthew comments that the symbol of night 'is able to carry humanity's pain, able to hold even such a sense of alienation from God that the inner self feels dismantled... (But) it is able also to hold the "spiritual resurrection".' Darkness is the time of 'letting God be who he is' (Matthew 1995, p.56). Communion with God is to be experienced through contemplation, which John describes as being 'naught else than a secret, peaceful and loving infusion from God, which, if it is permitted, enkindles the soul with the spirit of love'

(St John of the Cross, 2003, p.27; Book 1, Ch. 10, 6). This inrush of the God of love into our lives makes Matthew describe night as 'His love felt (by us) as pain' (Matthew 1995, p.57).

It seems that what John is saying is that night time can be regarded as that time when nothing happens, a kind of non-time. Or it can be a time when horrors that remain hidden during the day suddenly bubble to the surface. Or it can be a time of revelation. For many patients, coming into hospital can be a time of dislocation, a time when the normal bearings of life are thrown out of kilter and even lost touch with altogether. Because it is a time when patients are taken well outside their emotional, and spiritual as well as their physical, comfort zone, it can feel a very chaotic experience indeed. St John's idea is that for those *with* faith, this period of darkness can provide an opportunity for God's Spirit to fill our lives afresh. There is the sense that, for John, any dark experience can have a positive dimension for the person concerned. For those *without* faith, perhaps what John has to say is about simply being open to the possibility of something positive coming out of something negative. Being in a dark place of human experience certainly can change our sense of perspective with reference to what we regard as important or unimportant in our lives. At any time of disorientation, what can help us endure is the knowledge that we are not alone, that we have the offer of companionship, someone with whom we can share our worries, and who will accompany us through this experience. In hospital, this companion may be a family member or a friend, it may be a member of staff. John tells us that the ultimate companion in darkness is God himself beckoning us ever onward to new realizations, to new ways of interpreting reality in which each one of us is located.

The German theologian and Lutheran pastor Dietrich Bonhoeffer (1906–1945), speaking out of the dark experience of being imprisoned by the Nazis in 1943 for his part in a failed attempt to assassinate Hitler, comments that what compounded his dark experience was the uncertainty as to what the outcome of his period of incarceration might be. At times he believed that he would be released, at other times that he would die in prison. This uncertainty clearly shaped the writing of the letters he wrote in prison, as did the need to bolster the spiritual strength of those to whom he was writing. What Bonhoeffer advocates is 'living every day as if it were our last, and yet living in faith and responsibility as through there were to be a great future', whether in this life or the next (1971, p.15). Bonhoeffer's uncertainty as to what the outcome of his own incarceration might be resonates well with patients in hospital from the onset of their hospital admission (particularly for those who are emergency admissions) and continues to resonate with patients through every stage of their patient journey, both when they are waiting for a procedure to happen, or awaiting the results of any procedure. For the patient, the abiding question, with its subsidiary, is 'Will I be able to carry on as before or is there to be a change as to how I live my life day by day? What might be the new rules of engagement?' Patients vary as to how they deal with this uncertainty. Some will find themselves disabled by uncertainty and require much support; others, like Bonhoeffer, will worry about the effects that this uncertainty may have on their nearest and dearest.

PATIENT EXPERIENCE

Within a few months of being appointed to my hospital chaplaincy post, I was called to Intensive Care in the middle of the night by the ward sister to see a member of staff. The nurse in question seemed to be having some kind of breakdown. Alone with her in the relatives' room, there were periods where we sat in silence and when she talked and cried. Things were going wrong in her family. She seemed to be having a crisis in her faith, having been all her life a devout Roman Catholic. She was finding it hard to pray, because she wasn't sure where God was for her any more. I asked her whether she had any sense of there being a light shining in her darkness. She said that she could see no light at all. But in the darkness she did admit to sensing a benign presence. The darkness, although being total and very real, did not for her signify a total absence of God. The realization that God was in her darkness, as she was to tell me some months later, was the beginning of that member of staff's journey back to faith.

Suffering

For St John of the Cross, suffering is seen as growing pains, maturation accompanying a period of growth. John uses the picture of a mother's evolving relationship with her child to make this point, which Matthew summarizes as 'a mother weaning a child so he may grow; a mother picking up a child, so he, and she, might actually get somewhere' (Matthew 1995, p.79). So Matthew would seem to be saying that, for John, suffering is not an example 'of God's withdrawal, but of his maternal love drawing closer' (p.80). Furthermore, 'it is when you understand him (God) less clearly, that you are coming closer to him' (Canticle 2nd redaction 1.12, cited in Matthew 1995, p.97). Be that as it may, that might not be how it is perceived by the sufferer themselves.

When one person's suffering is caused by the abuse of another, an abuse which has its origins in humanity's inhumanity to itself, how is one to proceed towards some kind of resolution, with perpetrator and victim being set free from that cycle of violence that has its roots in the constant need for revenge? The contemporary theologian Miroslav Volf (b. 1956), writing out of the Balkan conflict which lasted most of the 1990s (when what was the former Yugoslavia fragmented into Croatia, Serbia and Bosnia Herzegovina), seeking to address how he, a Croat, can ever forgive the atrocities perpetrated against his people by Serbians, is clear that the first step is to realize, and what's more acknowledge, that all of us are a mixture of good and bad, that we each have something of the other within ourselves.

This refusal to accept 'the mote in our own eye' for Volf means that the resulting 'chimeral goodness of the self is but the flip side of the evil that it projects onto others' (1996, p.79). No one therefore is entirely innocent of sin, not the perpetrators of guilt nor even their victims. Furthermore, although their sins cannot be understood to be of equal magnitude, 'intertwined through the wrongdoing committed and suffered, the victim and violator are bound in the tragic and self-perpetuating solidarity of sin' (p.82). This has implications for any third party looking on who can so easily either get drawn into attributing innocence or guilt or refuse to engage with the situation at all. There is no escape from what Volf terms 'non-innocence'. To help assuage the notion that 'in a world so manifestly drenched with evil, everybody is innocent in their own eyes' (p.79), Volf urges that there should be 'a judicious retrieval of the doctrine of original sin' (p.84).

Four years later, the British theologian Al McFadyen does just this when he looks again at the doctrine of sin, exploring what it has to say in the light of two extreme examples, namely the sexual abuse of children and the Holocaust. Before he considers these concrete examples, he seeks to discover afresh 'the language of "sin"' and explore why it 'has fallen largely into disuse in the general public (but also in much Christian and theological discourse) as a language for talking about the pathological in human affairs'. He wonders whether this might be, first, due to 'the secularization of our culture' with its emphasis on the individual rather than the communal dimension; second, because 'the suspicion that Christian understanding of sin might be counter moral and/or counter scientific'; or third, because of 'the suspicion that sin is a language of blame and condemnation', especially popular with religious people (McFadyen 2000, p.3). McFadyen defines sin as 'that which constricts and restricts human beings from the abundance and plenitude of being-in-relation which is proper to them' (p.162). It is 'a comprehensive turning away from God' (p.195). For McFadyen, rediscovering 'the language of "sin"' is vital, because he maintains that if we cannot speak of sin, we 'cannot speak of God in relation to the world' at all (p.4). 'The language of "sin"', because it is a God-related language, is thus inherently a theological language. As with all language, it can lose its cutting edge if it is employed over-specifically or over-generally. 'The language of "sin" can thus be demeaned 'by either restricting its use (to a religious enclave) or its referential range (to the private and personal)... Alternatively, its public meaning and reference might be secured by evaporating it of any distinctively theological reference and function' (p.5). McFadyen's concern is that our society has become secularist by default.

In exploring what lies at the root of sexual abuse, McFadyen understands this to be 'fundamentally an abuse of trust and power' (p.78). Because this distorts a child's ability in relating to those around them, it also affects how they perceive themselves, projecting themselves into a world of isolation and secrecy (p.61). Because invariably the child has been forced to keep the abuse secret (especially if the abuser is known to the child), McFadyen believes the child feels that as 'I am in control of the secret and fear its exposure, then I must be responsible for the abuse'. So on top of the original abuse is heaped 'traumatic sexualisation...betrayal... powerlessness...(and) stigmatisation' (p.73). In all probability such profound damage may well stay with the abused well into adult life and may never be fully healed. Allowances must be made for those who have been abused making bad choices into adult life. Rather than being capable of free will, they are only able to exercise 'bound will'. Furthermore, McFadyen is clear that 'If we are unable adequately to name the personal pathological in which we participate, we cannot be personally accountable for them before God' (p.129). This raises the very interesting issue of the culpability of those abusers who have been abused themselves.

The abuse of the Jews and other perceived marginal groups by the Nazis arose out of their desire for perfect nationhood which they saw in absolute and exclusivist terms. Whereas originally Jews by their Jewishness helped give a sense of identity to those who were not Jewish in their un-Jewishness, it was but a small step to see those who were different to the host community, by their very existence, representing a threat to it, and therefore to them being demonized. The Nazi mindset began this process by depersonalization, 'relativising personal identity to that of the group' (McFadyen 2000, p.242). It interfered with anything that enabled the 'celebration of personal, cultural and religious identities' (p.243). Thus, it was able to perceive that 'Jews were weeds or cancerous cells threatening the integrity of (racially ordered) social organisms, rather than social organisms with their own, particular integrity' (p.241). And, the persecution of Jews and other groups of perceived 'different' people 'was a means of energising and securing German identity' (p.241). The cold logic of Nazism could only see this securing of identity being achieved by the elimination and extermination of all opposition.

For Volf, the question that needs addressing is not how does one eliminate difference, but how does one live fully with it. How can one 'live with integrity and...bring healing to a world of inescapable non-innocence that often parades as its opposite' (Volf 1996, p.84)? The answer which he gives is that 'we should demask as inescapably sinful the world constructed around exclusive moral polarities...and then seek to transform the world...guided by the recognition that the economy of undeserved grace has primacy over the economy of the moral desert' (pp.84–5). And yet we are so easily 'lured' by the former, having as it does the appearance of 'a wolf dressed up in sheep's clothing'. Volf wonders whether our being drawn towards this polarity has something to do with us being anxious about our mortality, survival, even our very identity, and the necessity of marking out for ourselves very clear boundaries or rules of engagement. So, 'instead of reconfiguring myself to make space for the other, I seek to reshape the other into who I want her to be in order that in relation to her, I may be who I want to be' (p.91). But in those who have consistently been abused, the opposite can also be the case in which there is effectively 'exclusion of the self from the will to be oneself' (p.91).

In examining how we might relate with one another, Volf takes as his model 'God's reception of hostile humanity into divine communion' (p.100). This immediately shifts the focus from how the oppressed (and the oppressor) can find liberation as an end in itself, to one of loving relationship. Following the thinking of the liberation theologian Gustavo Gutiérrez (b.1928), Volf says that the 'deepest root of all servitude is the breaking of friendship with God and with other human beings, and therefore cannot be eradicated except by the unmerited redemptive love of the Lord whom we receive by faith and in communion with one another' (p.100).

Volf's work in particular challenges hospital chaplains to help patients understand, reinforced by the chaplains' ministry of presence at the bedside (and by inclusive passages of scripture and by such poems as 'Footprints'), that God is alongside us, indeed within us; that just as God has space in his heart for us, so may we find space in our hearts for God.

PATIENT EXPERIENCE

When a patient's reality is a world of pain and suffering, there is always the danger of those who are well forgetting the reality of the unwell. It is relatively easy to speak of suffering leading to spiritual growth if one is not actually suffering oneself. To talk of suffering being an indication of 'a function of sin' in the world certainly at one level needs to be roundly challenged, lest the patient somehow thinks that their suffering is a punishment for past wrongdoing (and what that would say about the kind of God who would use suffering as a form of punishment). But the power games that can be played in any institution, with those who have knowledge exercising inappropriate power over those who do not, certainly does need to be challenged within the healthcare environment. This includes any kind of obvious mental, emotional and physical abuse. But it also includes those more insidious actions where patients are known by their illnesses rather than by their names; where patients (and their relatives if appropriate) are not fully consulted as to their treatment; where elderly patients in need of social care are made to feel guilty because they are perceived as 'bed blockers'; where patients suffering from dementia are not provided with sufficient help and care in busy ward settings. A very important tool in the patient's spiritual armoury can be their stubbornness, sheer bloody-mindedness and refusal to give up.

Surviving

How are people enabled to survive periods of darkness in their lives? Bonhoeffer, for example, approached his enforced imprisonment by treating it as an extended sabbatical, 'a good spiritual Turkish bath' (1971, p.22); as an opportunity for study in an attempt to normalize the abnormal; and so he craved books and intellectual conversation. He was also buoyed up by glimpses of the outside world: sunlight, the stars, a bird singing, the ringing of a church bell. Furthermore, despite being denied the sacraments of the Church and the physical fellowship of other Christians, the Church's year, especially its feast days, also gave a structure to his imprisonment, certain periods seeming more poignant than others. Aspects of the Church's liturgy were also important, as was reading the Bible, which he attempted to do 'straight through from cover to cover' (the book of Job carrying a special resonance), and singing psalms and hymns (p.40). And then there were the reflections that flowed from this. Ten days into his imprisonment, on 25 April 1943, was Easter Day. He wrote to his parents, 'Good Friday and Easter free us to think about the other things far beyond our present fate, about the ultimate meaning of all life, suffering and events. And we lay hold of a great hope' (p.22); a topic given added weight by his situation. On another occasion, Whit Sunday 1943, when he had been two months in prison, he contrasted the sound of Babel and Pentecost with the silence of his prison cell. Another way that Bonhoeffer strove to keep a positive frame of mind was by pleading the justness of his cause such as in his letters to the Judge Advocate (pp.64–9).

For Bonhoeffer, it was also important to receive news of his family and friends; 25 April was also the birthday of his fiancée. He imagined conversations with them, their wellbeing or otherwise, concerts they had been to which he had imagined attending in his mind, sometimes confirmed in future correspondence and rare visits. In a letter to his parents, he acknowledged himself that:

> [i]n general, a prisoner is no doubt inclined to make up, through exaggerated sentimentality, for the soullessness and lack of warmth of his surroundings... The right thing for him to do then is to call himself to order with a cold shower of common sense and humour. (p.71)

For Bonhoeffer, *'the great thing is to stick to what one still has and can do...and not to be dominated by the thought of what one cannot do, and by the feelings of resentment and discontent'* (pp.38–9; emphasis added).

For Volf, a major help in surviving the suffering of ethnic persecution is to have an awareness that life can recover a sense of meaningfulness. For him in his particular situation, that which gives life meaning is rooted in how reconciliation can become a reality for those who appear to represent irreconcilable positions. It involves first seeking to discover and then embracing the otherness of God. One cannot begin to embrace the otherness of God unless one acknowledges the importance of difference. Any attempt to reconcile those whose differences have not been acknowledged and worked through will remain stillborn. Furthermore, how we view otherness is intricately bound up with how we regard our own sense of identity. For Volf, 'the future of our world will depend on how we deal with identity and difference' (1996, p.20). Key to this discussion is exploring 'what kind of selves we need to be in order to live in harmony with others' (p.20). And what is the role of the gospel narrative in all this? Volf is clear that it would be a mistake to leave the gospel narrative behind in an attempt to be ethically relevant now. What is required is finding a way of re-inhabiting these stories in the light of where we are today.

And yet there is also a role, Volf believes, for a kind of active forgetting, a letting go of those prejudices which imprison us so that the healing of past memories can take place For, he says:

> if we must remember wrongdoings in order to be safe in an unsafe world, we must also let go of the memory in order to be finally redeemed… Only those who are willing ultimately to forget will be able to remember rightly. (p.132)

This active forgetting can only take place 'in the arms of God in a divine embrace' (pp.134–5). And this model for active forgetting is God. Volf believes that 'God forgets humanity's sins in the same way God forgives humanity's sins by taking sins away from humanity and placing them upon God-self' (p.140). For Volf:

> [t]he cross of Christ should teach us that the only alternative to violence is self-giving love, willingness to absorb violence in order to embrace the other in the knowledge that truth and justice have been, and will be upheld by God. (p.296)

Viktor Frankl (1905–1997), a psychologist, who was imprisoned in a concentration camp during the Second World War by the Nazis, used the experience to reflect from inside this 'psychological experiment' how prisoners, including himself, survived their incarceration. He observed that they seemed to pass through three stages in an attempt to process their experience from initial imprisonment to liberation (for those who were liberated). 'The period following his admission' was characterized by 'shock'; 'the period when he is well entrenched in camp routine' by 'apathy' 'and the period following his release and liberation' by sheer 'disbelief' (Frankl 1946, p.6ff). Unsurprisingly, he spends most time looking at the second stage, the stage we might describe as that of institutionalization. There seems to have been a conscious decision on behalf of some prison guards to break prisoners' wills, sometimes overtly by beating them into submission, and more covertly by depriving prisoners of the best of the paltry food rations; and in the way they treated the sick and the dying who were regarded as perfectly expendable commodities. As a fellow prisoner, Frankl comments, 'All we possessed was our naked existence' and the ability to 'choose one's attributes in a given set of circumstances, to choose one's own way' (pp.13, 65). Understandably, saving one's own skin was foremost in a prisoner's survival toolkit. This was made all the easier by a complete 'lack of sentiment' both to one another and to the outside world. Frankl observes that there was no talk of cultural matters other than politics or religion (pp.32, 33). It is as though awareness of the higher human qualities would underline the depravity of prisoners' day-to-day existence.

> And yet, talk of religion, was the most sincere imaginable... The depth and vigour of religious belief often surprised and moved a new arrival. Most impressive in this connection were improvised prayers or services in the corner of a hut, or in the locked cattle truck in which we were brought back from a distant work site... In spite of all the enforced physical and mental primitiveness of the life in a concentration camp, it was possible for spiritual life to deepen. (p.33)

It is as though people who suffered outwardly 'were able to retreat from their terrible surroundings to a life of inner riches and spiritual freedom' (p.35). Related to this religiously spiritual world was the calling into one's mind one's loved ones. He comments:

> I understand how a man who has nothing left in the world still may know bliss, be it only for a brief moment, in the contemplation of his beloved... Love goes very far beyond the physical person of the beloved. It finds its deeper meaning in his spiritual being, his inner self. (p.36)

Whether they are physically present or not 'ceases somehow to be of importance' (p.37). For Frankl, 'love is the ultimate and the highest goal to which man can aspire... The salvation of man is through love and in love' (p.36).

Frankl talks of the importance of developing a sense of humour, which he sees as 'some kind of trick learned whilst masking the art of living' (p.43). He gives the example of the more privileged prisoners from time to time improvising 'a kind of cabaret', which was so valued 'that a few ordinary prisoners went to see the cabaret in spite of their fatigue, even though they missed their daily portion of food by going'. At the end of the day, humour was another of the soul's weapons in the fight for self-preservation – 'sometimes it quite literally could save your life if you clapped those prisoners who were the guards' informants' (p.43). Frankl tells of camp life having to be lived in the present, in the immediate, the 'now'. 'Everything that was not connected with the immediate task of keeping oneself and one's closest friends alive lost its value' (p.49). So, for example, prisoners would take the clothes of sick patients if these were better than their own. To keep oneself 'safe' at Auschwitz, a prisoner 'generally answered all questions truthfully but…was silent about anything that was not expressly asked for' (p.53). Not being noticed was key to surviving.

PATIENT EXPERIENCE

If the patient is well enough, one way of transforming their stay in hospital in an attempt to normalize the abnormal is to treat it like a holiday from work. Another is to make sure that they can see the outside world. Corner beds by windows have the effect of putting a person's healthcare worries into perspective. Having some kind of structure to the day, whether that is self-imposed or dictated by the hospital environment in which one finds oneself, can mark out one's hospital stay in a more manageable way. Being able to communicate with the outside world (without it costing the world) can be similarly transformative.

Patients in hospital may also be aware of the different world views of health and wholeness that seem irreconcilable one with another, which they can experience as a result of their hospitalization. And which is the right one – the medical, the social, the political, the financial or the holistic model? There needs to be an understanding that those working in healthcare can have a different understanding of certain terms to that of the patients in their care. Perhaps what is needed is a revisiting of those models of healthcare that put the patient at the centre of care and an active forgetting of those that do not, and to be ever watchful that patients and staff understand what each is saying to the other.

In hospital, institutionalization can establish itself very quickly too. For then, after the 'shock' of admission, can come, if not 'apathy', the desire to play the game. After a long admission there can be 'disbelief' that the time has come to go home. For patients who have undergone particularly critical episodes, there can be 'disbelief' that they are still alive. But so too can come the opposite of these three qualities: relief to come into hospital in the first place, frustration that one is still there, and a hurry to leave, sometimes leading patients to discharge themselves, clearly not an option within the context of prison life. That which sustains patients in hospital is also the love of those close to them, the practice of a religion, being able to look out of the window, reading or listening to music. The use of humour can also take away the emotive power of the illness without necessarily affecting its outcome (such as giving your stomach bag, drip stand or drain a name, for example). But there will also occasionally be those patients who cut themselves off from other human contact and from the rest of the world, enduring their illness in self-imposed isolation. Of particular relevance to those patients suffering from life-limiting illness is the importance of life having to be lived in the present, as one of the by-products that such a diagnosis can instil is a reassessment of their perception of time. Whilst dwelling in the past is still possible, making plans for the distant future is not. And preoccupation with the past is frowned upon if it is seen as wasting time. Living fully in the present (or more fully than before receiving their diagnosis) also serves to bring greater intensity to the inner life of the patient. A sense of hope is paramount. Not false hope that has no basis in reality, but hope in that which can be achieved, such as a chance to recuperate with family and friends when discharged from hospital, a weekend's home leave, going on that dream holiday NOW, a peaceful death, a belief in a faith which through time and across the world has sustained and continues to sustain the living and departed.

Conclusion

At the heart of this chapter has been the process of engaging in 'critical dialogue' between 'theological norms' supported by historical examples of literal and metaphorical imprisonment, and reflecting upon whether these offer any illumination to the 'contemporary experience' of hospitalization and the restrictions that patients can feel placed upon them when their freedom of movement and/or daily routine is changed by being hospitalized or by having to process a serious illness or disability. Pervading the darkness that suffering can engender has been the realization that suffering exists because it seems to be an integral by-product of the world as it has been created. Glimpsing the hope that survival can herald, without in any way believing that 'God…actually arranges that some people suffer more than others because it is part of his great cosmic plan', there has also been the acknowledgement that even when there is no initial sense of the presence of God – indeed, rather his absence – the presence of the chaplain has the potential to affirm that 'God is somehow involved in every person's life' (Cassidy 1988, pp.156–7).

2

LISTENING TO THE VOICE
OF CLINICAL EXPERIENCE
Surviving the Darkness of Hospitalization

This chapter continues the process of engaging in 'critical dialogue between theological norms and contemporary experience' (Pattison and Lynch 2005, pp.410–11) and explores whether this position can be supported by examples taken from a clinical perspective.

An approach will be employed in which relevant case studies, drawn from my own praxis, will be considered, in the light of relevant literature concerned with difficult experiences that can be encountered within the healthcare setting. The areas I shall explore will include: end-of-life care, bereavement, loss (suffered by individuals and groups), disability and dementia. The conversation partners I shall engage with are: the psychiatrists Elizabeth Kübler-Ross, Colin Murray Parkes and therapist Robert Weiss, the writer and former hospital chaplain Peter Speck, the psychoanalyst Edward Shapiro, the writer and former Dean of Westminster Abbey Wesley Carr; David Pailin, the father of a short-lived disabled baby, Nancy Eiesland, a writer who is herself disabled, Christine Bryden, a writer who is living with a dementia diagnosis, the writer and former hospice chaplain Malcolm Goldsmith and Suzanne McDonald. As was noted in the previous chapter, for those people of faith looking to survive periods of suffering, there remains the parallel problem of sensing or not sensing the presence or absence of God within the healthcare environment.

Case study 1: Being diagnosed with a life-limiting illness

T was a middle-aged male Motor Neurone Disease (MND) patient who came on to the ward at the local hospice. He had been an extremely active man, serving as a police officer, and had done a lot of football coaching with youngsters. He felt very deeply the unfairness of this illness, which he described as living hell. Since his diagnosis, the patient had thrown himself into fundraising for the Motor Neurone Disease Association (one event of which involved people sponsoring plastic ducks racing down a river). These fundraising activities culminated in him being sponsored to walk the Normandy beaches with his best friends, which was videoed for posterity.

When he began what turned out to be his final stay at the hospice (which lasted a number of weeks), his room (which is specially designed with MND patients in mind) had his name on the door. It became an extension of his home, with family and friends coming and going most of the time. His personality dominated the room. It became a place where staff dropped in to be cheered up. He insisted on being the person that he had always been, who just happened to be ill. Having checked with the staff first, friends would 'kidnap' him and take him off to football matches or to the pub, where he could have a drink with his friends. They continued to drop by, even when he became too ill to leave the hospice.

Throughout his life, T had faced difficult situations head on. With the chaplains, he became keen to write his own funeral eulogy. He wanted to complete this not just before he died, but before he could no longer talk. This was honed over many weeks. As I was the chaplain on duty when he died, the family asked if I would deliver this eulogy at his funeral. Despite some rather 'rich' language, it was read word for word as he had intended.

REFLECTION

Within the context of healthcare, one comes face to face with the reality of loss in all its nakedness, starkness and unavoidability, when a patient is diagnosed with a life-limiting illness in which, maybe for the very first time, they begin to realize that life itself is a terminal condition. Most patients in hospital look forward to a time of full or partial recovery. A patient with a life-limiting illness has to try to begin to make sense of a world view in which this will not be true for them. They may be helped through various crises, but their underlying prognosis will not improve and will eventually deteriorate. Kübler-Ross has sought to describe the process that a patient undergoes in seeking to adjust to this new dispensation. Whilst clearly not everybody reacts to a difficult diagnosis in the same way, she discerned four key stages through which people pass. These are denial, bargaining, depression and acceptance. Although, in describing them, the appearance can be given of a linear journey travelling in one direction, Kübler-Ross (1970) herself points out that this is usually not the case. People can become stuck, go backwards, have several goes at a stage, almost needing to build up a physical momentum in order to move on to the next stage.

When a patient first becomes aware that they have a life-limiting illness, the shock can cause them to go into *denial (1)*. Kübler-Ross believes this to be no bad thing as she believes that 'the need for denial exists in every patient', giving space for the information to be digested and in time, absorbed (p.37). But during this information digestion process, the patient may vent their frustration on anybody close at hand, even on themselves. Kübler-Ross observes that 'grief, shame and guilt are not very far from feelings of anger and rage' (p.4). But if no overt anger is expressed, there can be a real worry that the person has not yet faced up to their own mortality. And then the *bargaining (2)* begins as the patient can fall back on notions of reward and punishment so prevalent in childhood. The patient believes that:

> there is a slim chance that he (she) may be rewarded for good behaviour and be granted a wish for special services. His (her) wish is most always an extension of life, followed by the wish for a few days without pain. (p.73)

When the bargaining doesn't work, and the stark reality of the patient's situation becomes overtly apparent, a factor which can render a person physically, mentally and spiritually exhausted, a patient can become extremely *depressed (3),* both in response to the bad news itself and the loss that their death will presage. But Kübler-Ross believes that:

> If a patient has had enough time…and has been given some help in working through the previously described stages, he (she) will reach a stage during which he (she) is neither depressed nor angry about his (her) fate. (p.99)

And only then can the final stage of *acceptance (4)* be deemed to have been reached (with the proviso that people can still regress to earlier stages).

What is vital for the patient in this whole process is the keeping alive of hope. This is achieved through the quality of the interaction of the carer with the patient which, whether articulated or not, is one way in which that patient can sense the presence of God. If a patient is not loved, or if their loved ones have given up on them, the very real impression is given to the patient that 'slowly but surely he (she) is beginning to be treated like a thing' (p.99). Socially, they will feel that they have already died.

Case study 2: Grieving the loss of a loved one

C was an eight-year-old girl who died on the children's ward nine months after I became chaplain at my present hospital. She had been diagnosed with a type of bone cancer some months before and was well known to the community paediatric team. During the course of her illness one of her legs had been amputated in an attempt to stop her cancer from spreading. Stabilized by medication, she was able to travel to Disneyland in Florida, so that she could 'swim with the dolphins'. It was there that her final healthcare crisis began, involving her being intubated and flown back to the UK and, at the parents' request, being transferred to the Island. As I was with her parents and C when she died, I was asked to take her funeral. When I undertook the pre-funeral visit at the family home, it became clear that C's father was very bitter at his daughter's death. He placed C's prosthetic leg on my lap and was insistent on showing me C's hair, which the parents had kept when she lost it through her chemotherapy.

She was one of four children diagnosed with cancer in the hospital's catchment area in a very short space of time. Because they became friends, so too did their parents. One child had died before C, one died shortly afterwards and one is still alive. These last two children attended C's funeral. The four families remained very angry at the diagnosis of the children's cancers. They were convinced there must be a common cause. When this was not found to be the case, the parents' anger increased. A clinical psychologist was brought in by the hospital to help this group of parents work through their grief. He involved me to see if there might be a way in which this grief could be worked through symbolically in worship. This led to the setting up of the first children's memorial service with these bereaved parents becoming the planning group for this event. C's family have attended most of these. C's family also established a memorial garden at C's school where all children at the school now have access to a quiet and reflective space.

REFLECTION

A direct parallel to trying to come to terms with being diagnosed with a life-limiting illness is the experience of knowing that a loved one will die or has recently died. Parkes and Weiss have observed that people seem to respond differently to bereavement. 'Some recover from grief unscathed, or even strengthened, while others suffer lasting damage to body, mind or spirit' (1983, p.ix). Key to how a person grieves is the importance 'of the value of preparation in dealing with inescapable pain and loss' (p.255). As we shall see below, this is also acknowledged by Speck (1978). As Kübler-Ross observed with terminally ill patients, people need time to adjust to their newly bereaved (or soon to be bereaved) condition. 'They must first be given support and time to grieve for the loss of the cherished past' (Parkes and Weiss 1983, p.255).

When a person grieves, whether it represents 'a struggle between opposing impulses, one tending towards realization of the loss, the other towards retention of the object', or represents a constant looking for the one that is lost (p.2), Parkes and Weiss are clear that grief is normative at the death of a loved one; it is the 'absence of grief' that is not (p.2). Elsewhere Parkes has written that 'grief is a process'. Mirroring Kübler-Ross's grief stages of denial, bargaining, depression and acceptance, he identifies the phases of grief as 'numbness...pining...disorganization and despair...recovery'. Like her, he recognized that people 'can move back and forth through the phases' (1996, p.7). Some people clearly find it hard to begin the grieving process. This Parkes and Weiss refer to as 'pathological grief'. This can be observed when there has been 'sudden unexpected bereavement, a reaction of anger and/or self-reproach (ambivalence) against the deceased...intense yearning, often associated with a supposedly dependent relationship' (1983, p.52). That which is important in having a bearing on when grieving can begin is 'the mode of death...the types of social support that are available...(and) the predisposition of the bereaved (e.g. their age)' (pp.17–18). That which has a bearing on when grieving can draw to its close is 'the nature of the relationship with the person who has died, the personality of the survivor...(and) the surrounding social circumstances' (pp.19–20). Yet others can be so well prepared before their loved one's death that they want them to get on and die! As Parkes and Weiss warn us, '[i]t is sometimes tempting for us to want to put patients out of *our* misery' (p.256; emphasis added). But the greatest amount of preparation can't eliminate totally the trauma felt by the loss of a loved one when they have actually died.

The grief that C's family members felt at the death of their child was the last of a number of losses they had had to see her endure (and because of their love for her, endure themselves): the loss of her health, her hair, her leg (and therefore her mobility), her dream holiday and finally her life. Their grief manifested itself as a struggle between unspeakable sadness, naked anger and self-reproach for not being able to prevent her death, compounded by the grief that other families felt at the death (or likely death) of their children through cancer. A question that has remained unanswered is whether the establishment of the annual children memorial services has helped or hindered the grieving process for C's family and the families of her three friends. It has certainly helped to dissipate their initial anger. It has provided a framework in which C and other children who have died can be remembered and affirms that they will never be forgotten. Is it helping these families move on through their grief? Or is the danger that every year, as the same wounds of grief are reopened, the families are doomed to go round and round in circles? Because these services are rooted in a world faith (in this case the Christian faith), there is a sense in which those who are grieving are held in loving relationship with others who are grieving and with the source of life in all its fullness (whether overtly acknowledged as God or not) wherein lies the possibility of transformation.

Case study 3: Loss in other areas of healthcare

S, an active woman in her sixties, began her hospital stay in a six-bedded bay on one of the orthopaedic wards. She came in for a standard knee replacement operation. Post-operatively, she picked up an infection on her knee which was initially treated with drugs. Because of her infection she was moved to a single room on the same ward and was barrier nursed. Her physical and psychological condition deteriorated. Having thought she was coming into hospital to have an operation that would help improve her walking, S now found herself bed-bound and totally dependent on others. She had a strong Christian faith. It was important for her to receive Holy Communion weekly. This was brought to her by one of the hospital chaplains. As well as receiving the sacrament, this provided her with a regular opportunity to talk with a chaplain. It seemed to be important for S to be able to talk about how she was feeling to someone who was not a nurse or other clinical colleague for fear of taking up too much of their time; and someone who was not a member of her family for fear of upsetting them. Her conversation was full of questions: 'Why me?' 'What have I done to deserve this?' 'Is God testing me?'

Because her leg was continuing to deteriorate, her clinical team took the decision that in order to save her life, they would advise her to have a partial amputation. S was adamant that she would not have the operation. The family found this very hard to cope with and so over time felt duty-bound to try to change her mind. Eventually,

S acquiesced and agreed to the operation. Her physical health improved, and she was moved to the rehabilitation ward, where she remained for many weeks. When she was getting ready to leave the hospital, when asked by a chaplain how she was feeling now, S admitted very quietly that she had made the wrong decision about having the operation.

REFLECTION

Bereavement is not the only form of loss, whether it is expected or unexpected. Speck has looked at specific losses that occur within healthcare. The very fact of coming into hospital is itself a loss, whether the admission is planned or unexpected. There can be a loss of freedom of movement and of action; one's autonomy can be compromised; one can quickly become dependent on others for one's most basic needs. With this environment of loss can come other losses. Speck has helpfully indicated what these might be. Within obstetrics and gynaecology these can include 'spontaneous abortion and miscarriage or still-birth...infertility...congenital abnormality... menopause...hysterectomy' (1978, pp.33–52). Within general surgery loss can include 'mastectomy...colostomy...mutilation resulting from injury/surgery...amputation' (pp.53–76). Speck stresses the importance for a patient to 'be able to recognize his or her body image', as disfigurement 'can lead to stigmatization'. Surgery can result in a 'loss of self-esteem' for patients, so it is vital that not only the staff but also the family and friends can give them a sense of affirmation (p.76). For:

> if the patient enjoys secure and loving relationships in which he or she knows that it is not physical appearance, ability or prowess that is the relationship, then he or she will be more able to resolve the feelings generated by the loss. But one needs to bear in mind that a loss may seem the same for several patients but the significance of that loss will vary from person to person. (pp.76–7)

Then there is the sense of loss which is derived from a medical condition which Speck helpfully lists as including: 'loss of vision...loss of hearing...Chronic Bronchitis...Asthma... Multiple Sclerosis...Epilepsy...Osteoarthritis...degenerative disc disease and Rheumatoid arthritis...cardiac failure... stroke' (p.81). Some of these conditions are related to the general ageing process which can of itself also be perceived as loss. These illnesses 'often include the loss of independence, usefulness and purpose'. For the younger patient, there may be 'loss of employment' and a 'change of status' – from able-bodied to 'unemployable'. As with post-surgical patients, 'a positive and supportive approach to such patients with continuing encouragement, can lead to them adopting a reasonably active life style within the limits imposed by their illness' (p.110).

For S, her physical disfigurement was mirrored by a sense of spiritual disfigurement. Being denied adequate 'worrying time', Job-like, she could not begin to process why God had allowed this to happen to her, but she never doubted that God existed. Her regular receiving of Holy Communion and her contact with the chaplaincy team seemed to give her something to hang on to in the mist of her personal hell. Despite being a member of a loving family, S seemed to find it impossible 'to recognize her new body image', believing that she had been not just stigmatized but violated as a result of the operation (p.76). Her spiritual situation remained unresolved when she left the hospital.

Case study 4: Psycho-social transition

A is a young woman in her early twenties, who was a patient in the mental unit at my hospital. She began her stay on an open ward, but because she attempted suicide, she was moved to the locked ward, moving to the open ward just before she left hospital. She was hospitalized from April to December 2008. She believed that her mental health problems dated from the time that she came into hospital as a child aged 13, suffering from peritonitis. Whilst she never spoke specifically of what caused this incident, she was repeatedly abused by both parents as a child. She talked of praying to her womb, to her seed. She was very loath to speak of her family at all. Stable factors in her life were her late grandparents, who read her stories and also provided some kind of church connection. During her stay in the mental health unit, she read much Scripture and other religious material, and she regularly received Holy Communion from which she seemed to derive great solace and peace. She was extremely chaotic, both in her in her spiritual and day-to-day life. She seemed confused and found it very hard to make choices. She believed in Spirit guides, astral planes and the healing power of crystals. She imagined God to be a person, but also a ball of energy. She was concerned to know how you can know God is with you, feeling that if she cannot feel God close, he cannot be close. During her hospital stay, A had a way of pathologizing metaphors, reading herself into them. She began to use the medium of metaphor rooted in Scripture and elsewhere to communicate externally the chaos of her internal world, most particularly that of water. She longed for the spirit of God to move upon the face of her waters (Genesis 1.2). She mentioned Jesus stilling the storm and there being a sense of peace (Luke 8.22–5) and also talked of water as life-giving and God being in the water. She talked of the power of water, of herself 'bursting through the walls, bursting through the astral plane to freedom'. She read the Exodus account of Moses delivering the children of Israel out of slavery, which, of course, begins with crossing water (Exodus 14.15–31). She seemed to see this metaphor of journeying through wilderness to the Promised Land and back again as her story.

REFLECTION

Parkes has extended his work on bereavement to include psychosocial transitions, which, as he points out, 'are not confined to bereavement, they take place whenever we are faced with the need to make changes to our assumptions about the world' (1996, p.90). They also have a direct effect upon how we view ourselves. When a loved one dies, or is lost in some other way to us, not just one assumption but 'a whole set of assumptions about the world that relied upon the other person for their validity are suddenly invalidated' (p.90). Parkes believes that what has to happen at such a time as this is that we 'need to give up one set of habits (many of which may be so well established that they have become virtually automatic) in order to develop another' (p.90). Problems arise in this process of adaption, Parkes believes, when what 'is' gets out of step with what 'should be' (p.91).

Parkes identifies four possible changes of roles as being likely to take place. He lists these as follows:

1. The roles and functions previously performed by the missing member may remain unperformed.

2. A substitute for the missing member may be obtained from outside the family.

3. The roles of the missing member may be taken over by other family members.

4. The social system may break up.

(1996, p.100)

Parkes observes that not only a person's 'role' but also their 'bodily characteristics' and behaviour can all 'be affected by major loss such as bereavement' (p.94). And, he believes, 'change in the world's view of me are likely to be associated with changes in my view of myself' (p.97). The question which each of us has to ask ourselves when we find ourselves in a situation of loss is 'Who is the real me? Am I the person I believe myself to be or the person the world believes me to be? Is there an essential, unalterable me?' (p.98). Working through the grieving process, if it is to find any kind of resolution, demands nothing short of re-creation.

In various encounters with A, two things stand out. These are, first, the contrast in A's behaviour between the chaos of her day to day life and the outward and, as far as I can judge, inner peace that she exhibits after receiving the sacraments; and second, the use of the metaphor of water to speak to that chaos and the ever-present possibility of new beginnings. This would seem to echo John Foskett's (1984) theme of revelation rather than healing, as he imagines 'God going on manoeuvres' in the wilderness of mental illness. So in the midst of her chaos, is A showing us something new or, at the very least, something in a new light?

After A left the hospital, she was only at home briefly before she was re-admitted, with the self-same problems recurring. It appears that, for A, being in a semi-perpetual state of chaos is the norm, with periods of peace becoming almost aberrations. But if this is true, wherein lies hope, wherein dwells the divine? Hope lies, as the divine is manifested, in A's encounter with others, including chaplains, who care enough to listen and to journey with A through her darkness. Hope also lies in the belief that 'there is somewhere to go...that only he (God) can take us there' (Matthew 1995, p.57), that in the journeying and in the arriving, we are indeed 'cherished by God and will forever be embraced as a cherished part of the divine reality' (Pailin 1992, p.180).

Case study 5: Being lost in a familiar place

When I began working with my present Trust, in addition to the main district general hospital (DGH), there was a small cottage hospital housing around 20 patients situated about five miles away. Originally, this smaller hospital had had a maternity unit and carried out minor surgery. At the time I arrived, it specialized in two groups of patients: the frail elderly and those who had suffered brain damage through injury or genetic deterioration. A large percentage of this latter group was young middle-aged. Both groups of patients were effectively bed-bound. The staff who worked there were a dedicated team, many of whom had worked together over many years building up a special rapport not just with their patients but also with the relatives of those in their care. A decision was made to close this smaller hospital, and, despite much local protest, patients and staff were decamped to a new dedicated ward on the DGH site. The ward clerk's desk on the new unit continued to occupy the role it had in the cottage hospital, that of being the place where information could not only be disseminated but also gathered. Chaplaincy was involved in leading a service in the cottage hospital's chapel, giving thanks for what had been achieved, and looking forward, albeit with some trepidation, to what might be in the future.

Some two years after the transfer of these patients and staff to the DGH, a decision was taken to close this ward. The frail elderly were transferred to specialized nursing homes, the brain-damaged patients transferred to another ward on the DGH site, and, whilst no member of staff would be made redundant, the staff team was broken up. Managers did not often appear on the ward in person, preferring to communicate to staff either through the ward sister or through emails. Despite offers of support from occupational health, the chaplains found themselves supporting members of the team that was being broken up, because they were the ones that had an existing relationship with this team. They were the only ones who seemed to recognize that staff in their behaviour were exhibiting profound grief at the bereavement they were experiencing. Again the staff felt the need to mark that something very important in their lives was coming to an end. They decided to get together in a local pub for a 'wake'.

REFLECTION

Being lost in a familiar place can be more disturbing, more disorientating that being lost in an unfamiliar one. Within the hospital setting, it can apply to staff just as much as patients. It is not just that one's way of perceiving the world has been turned on its head, but that the vantage point from which one is making these observations has also disappeared. Being lost in this way can be experienced by individuals or groups, and within the healthcare environment by staff as well as patients. Shapiro and Carr (1991, pp.99–103) focus on staff members within organizations, either when change is introduced or when it needs to be introduced to remove bad practice and isn't. They point out that 'being lost in familiar places does not imply that men and women can do nothing other than acknowledge their feeling'. Feelings that can be experienced at such a time as this arise out of: not being part of the decision-making process that is initiating change and thus feeling excluded from it; being done to rather than consulted with (the inference being that staff have to 'either submit to the programme or protect themselves from it'); and not being clear as to the organization's task of which the current change (or lack of it) forms a part. The exclusion that some feel, at imposed change (or stasis), is compounded by those who are happy to embrace it with zeal and enthusiasm.

Despite this, Shapiro and Carr believe that with help, those who feel excluded 'can interpret the situation afresh', possibly through the use of 'interpretation free zones' (pp.145, 102). Rediscovering the art of interpretation is crucial in this process. Indeed, they have maintained that '[t]he uninterpreted space that is experienced between the individual and his social context is one of the main reasons for this experience being lost' (p.167). Failing to give sufficient attention to interpreting situations afresh serves to heighten the sense of disempowerment that they perceive to be common in society at large (p.180).

What help is there to enable either individuals or groups in this process of interpretation? Shapiro and Carr point out that faith groups have a role to play here as they believe that 'the social task of religious institutions is to enable individuals to face the connection between dependency and irrationality (as well as "illusion and delusion" (p.162)) by providing a managed and contained context for both' (p.159).

'Making connections' is a function that can also fall upon the faith professional such as a chaplain to facilitate. Religious institutions and facilitators are called upon to provide a 'holding environment' (which provides 'empathic interpretation and tolerance and containment' (p.36)), where difficult feelings 'can be addressed through ritualistic symbolic structure that enables chaotic experiences to be faced' (p.160). As Shapiro and Carr have observed, it seems that sometimes it is the presence and viewpoint of an outsider that acts as a catalyst for beginning the interpretative process. Within healthcare, this role may fall to the hospital chaplain.

It will be clear from the above that the group of staff in the case study suffered two bereavements, one following two years after the other, and arguably before the first had been satisfactorily processed by the staff concerned. Of the two, the second bereavement seemed to be the more traumatic for the staff, a change of personnel being far harder to cope with than a change of location. The second change was understood by ward staff quite simply as a betrayal of trust. Because managers were not often to be found on the ward, there was the perception by ward staff that they were not interested in what staff had to say to them, merely in communicating what managers had decided would happen to the staff. There seems to have been a singular failure in understanding the communal nature of the ward relationships. Many ward staff were not just ward colleagues but also friends. In assuring staff that no one would lose their jobs, but some of them would be redeployed, there was a lack of understanding that the ward unit as previously constituted was dying, and needed to be mourned. Because managers offered the staff no rite of passage, the staff evolved one of their own. Because of their anger, staff did not want a religious ritual. There may even have been a perception by some that God had deserted them at their moment of greatest need. But if this was the case, why did they want the chaplains to be present? Perhaps it was that the chaplains had a contextualising role, which enabled individuals who worked on that ward to embrace the unembraceable.

Case study 6: Disability

R1 was a man with profound learning disability who lived for nearly 20 years in the residential accommodation run by my Trust for this client group. Despite being physically unwell for many months, when R1 died in May 2010 aged 63, his death was sudden and unexpected. At the time of writing, whilst his mother is still alive, his father died in 2011, and because he had no other relatives, the staff at his home became by default his extended family. With R1's mother's permission, it was they who arranged his funeral service. They asked me to take his funeral as they wanted someone that both they and R1 knew. When I went on the funeral visit to meet with staff, what became very clear was how upset people were, not just present staff but staff who were no longer working at the Trust but had worked closely with R1 in the past. Despite R1 needing semi-constant care within the centre and when going on trips outside, his at times moody but often jovial nature (epitomized by a very wide and mischievous smile) communicated to staff the person within as opposed to the disability without. This was particularly felt by staff who had taken R1 on holiday, sometimes with other clients, sometimes by himself. Because his father had worked in the RAF, R1 was fascinated by planes and all kinds of transport. When he first met a person, as well as their name he wanted to know what car they drove. When staff went on holiday, they would always send him a card which invariably had some means of transport upon it. Because of the length of time R1 had been a resident at the centre, for many staff his death has felt like an end of a chapter. Because of changes in the provision of care for those with profound as well as less severe learning disability, and the belief in my Trust that this care should be individually rather than communally targeted and provided by social service rather than healthcare, the death of its longest-staying resident may, if not being the catalyst that enables this to happen, certainly come to symbolize the end of an era. Not only the staff but the other residents (some of whom attended R1's funeral) will feel this change very deeply.

REFLECTION

Along with Jean Vanier (2004), who was particularly interested in the relationship that is established between the disabled and able-bodied when living together in a community of love and mutual respect, two other key writers in this field have been Nancy L. Eiesland, a disabled person herself, and David A. Pailin, responding to the birth and short life of a severely disabled baby. Disablement, like beauty, would seem to be (to a greater or lesser extent) in the eye of the beholder, whether the 'beholder' is the disabled person themselves or someone else. It would seem to have an objective reality bound up with clinical symptoms and a subjective reality bound up with how the disability is perceived and experienced by the disabled person and society in general, a perception which in no small way is shaped by the symbolism in common parlance accompanying disablement and able-bodied-ness. Pailin warns that one must always beware of 'the error of judging other people's happiness and fulfilment in terms of what is appropriate for me' (1992, p.9). This can start to feel uncomfortable for those without marked disabilities, although people maybe disabled in non-physical and non-visible ways. If there is a perception that the able-bodied have value, are whole, have self-respect and self-esteem, there will inevitably be the sense for the disabled person that they are of little or of no value, damaged goods, lacking in self-respect and self-esteem, imprisoned. Even the very word 'disabled' itself would seem to define a person in the negative, in a way that, for example, the words 'differently abled' don't do.

In the light of the above, Eiesland believes that what is urgently required is nothing less than a resymbolization of how the disabled and able-bodied perceive themselves and one another. She believes that a way must be found in which able-bodied and disabled people alike discover a common humanity in which we only find completeness by exploring ways of 'holding our bodies together', a term she refers to as 'embodiment' (1994, p.95). And that requires a 'coming to terms with our own bodies'. For the disabled person, this means being able to accept their bodies as 'survivable' and as being 'painstakingly honestly and lovingly constructed' (p.96). The respect which comes from this acceptance is itself 'an act of resistance and liberation'. But as with all resymbolization, this can be 'both liberating for the marginalized group and unsettling for the dominant group' (p.96). Pailin succinctly believes that able-bodied and disabled people 'should be judged by how far they have realized their potentials rather than their success in satisfying some attainment targets' (pp.48–9). In other words, they should be driven by an internal rather than an external agenda.

One way that we can discover our common humanity is in the relationship that we have with God, born out of God's relationship with us. Whilst Vanier understands that 'true growth comes from God when we cry to him from the depths of the abyss to let his Spirit penetrate us' (1989, p.133), Pailin puts it thus:

> God cares for every person – in their pettiness and nastiness (which God wills to be transformed) as well as their love and creativity (which God desires to be enhanced)... God has the confidence to allow people to be themselves and to accept them for what they actually are. (1992, p.52)

We are forever 'embraced, cherished and valued by God'. The memory of each one of us is 'everlastingly preserved in the divine memory' (p.52).

It is impossible to conceive of R1 separate from his learning disability. As far as he was able, R1 seemed to live life to the full, helped in no small part by his dedicated carers. R1's world contained no artifice. When in his company, he demanded the whole of a carer's attention. But R1 was not just a person who received care; he was quite cable of giving care too. Staff had a great loyalty towards him. Within the Christian world view, the staff could be said to be enfleshing the love of God by having the confidence to allow people (in their care) to be themselves and to accept them for what they actually are (Pailin 1992, p.52). Staff have found themselves transformed by this process, because they have allowed themselves to face the essence of what 'human being-ness' actually means. In short, R1's vulnerability allowed staff to become vulnerable themselves as was borne out by the grief felt at R1's death.

Case study 7: Dementia

Every year at the Trust's assessment centre for those patients suffering with dementia, much is made of the annual Christmas carol service and Christmas party. This is an opportunity to celebrate all that this centre stands for, providing patients with a link with past Christmases and offering the possibility of re-membering memories that otherwise might remain lost. One year, when the respite role of the centre had become firmly established, a male patient, R2, and his wife attended the annual Christmas carol service and Christmas party. Before coming to be at this centre on this particular occasion, he had been in hospital on an older person's medical ward over a number of months. There his dementia had been diagnosed. He had been at this centre when it functioned as a respite centre. He had returned to have his deteriorating dementia assessed. R2 and his wife were sitting in the front row, and so I couldn't fail to notice them when taking the carol service. R2 had become very withdrawn and to all intents and purposes appeared to be asleep, until we sang the carol 'Away in a manger'. He began mouthing the words. When the carol ended, his word-mouthing ceased. In talking with R2's wife after the service, it became clear that she was very angry. This seemed to stem from the fact that because her husband was of West Indian origin and she was not, since their marriage at the end of the Second World War, she had experienced years of racial discrimination. Life for her had become one long fight, her husband's dementia being the final unfairness that life had thrust upon her, fuelled by the loss of the respite function of the centre she had come to know and trust. She dealt with it like she always dealt with difficulties, by fighting. Despite being back at this centre, no care would ever be good enough for her husband. The staff at times found her very difficult to deal with. A month after Christmas, R2 died. I conducted his funeral. Apart from his wife, it was members of staff who formed the rest of the congregation, having become by default their extended family.

REFLECTION

An initial reaction from those not suffering from dementia observing those who are can be to see a de-compositional process at work, to witness a journey from order into chaos, an un-creation. Goldsmith is one of a number of writers to offer a different perspective, believing that it is in the:

> very essence of the Christian faith that we discern the presence and activity of God in brokenness and weakness. It is when we are at the limits of our powers and strength that we allow God to break through our defences and to support and sustain us. (1998, p.8)

In a BBC Radio 4 *Thought for the Day*, from a relative's perspective, Samuel Wells, the vicar of St Martin-in-the-Fields in London, said something very similar.

> In the face of deficit, decline and death we want to keep as
> much of the person for as long as we can... But...maybe a
> better path lies in letting go, in letting loose, in allowing to
> roam free. If death is starting now, maybe resurrection can
> start now too. (2015)

So it is possible that those suffering from dementia have positive
as well as negative insights to share about the nature of what it
means to be human, and to say something of God's relationship
with his creation. Be that as it may, this in no way minimizes
the very real fear and anxiety that can be felt by the dementia
sufferer and their loved ones as they watch on helplessly at the
foot of their particular cross.

Christine Bryden, herself suffering from dementia, rather
than perceiving dementia as a fragmentation or an annihilation
of the self, sees it as a voyage of discovery. In quoting a fellow
dementia sufferer's response to her condition, she writes,
'I think the most releasing realization I came to early in my
journey with dementia was that the further I progressed with
the physical/psychological decline the more my spirit man
increased in proportion' (2005, p.161). Bryden even feels that,
as a result of her increasing dementia, 'I am becoming who I
really am' (p.162). She draws on insights from Viktor Frankl as
to how one might endure the trauma of dementia. 'For people
struggling with dementia, it is a similar path of survival, illusion,
denial, apathy, humour and a search for meaning' (p.162).

Drawing upon Israel's experience of exile in Babylon,
Goldsmith suggests that just as the Children of Israel came to
know God's presence in this unknown country, so too can the
patient suffering from dementia. Goldsmith also talks of people
'living in the "space" between crucifixion and resurrection'
(2004, p.206). Following in the footsteps of St John of the
Cross, McDonald believes, that in regarding this space as Holy
Saturday, the:

> 'empty' day between the cross and the resurrection,
> where apparent defeat is not immediately followed by

triumphant vindication, we are enabled, tentatively, to speak theologically of dementia... Holy Saturday shows us God in the emptiness and God taking the emptiness into himself. (2003, p.6)

One thing that is shared by, and unites, those suffering and those not suffering with dementia is the recognition 'that there is something within men and women which hints at or speaks of, that which is beyond them' (Goldsmith 2004, p.143). It is as though this is a gift that those with dementia give to the Church. So in coming alongside those with dementia, we can both feel their pain and become aware of our own vulnerability. This vulnerability can affect our theological thinking. If we are to engage honestly with those with dementia, our thinking must be rooted in 'a theology of patience, of suffering and of "failure". We need an open-ended, non-judgmental and merciful theology, not a theology of certainty, but of tentative exploration' (p.204).

There seems to be a marked difference between how the unit staff regard their patient guests and how the managers of the service regard them. Whereas the first seem to be concerned about quality of life experience, the second seem concerned with processing the maximum number of patients through the system. The annual Christmas carol service and Christmas party can thus be regarded as countercultural to, and undermining of, assessment centre philosophy, as it is not about seeing a fragmented or de-compositional process at work, but celebrating life in all its fullness. It is as though remembering one story, the Christmas story, is allowing the re-membering of others, 'the spirituality of religion' enabling 'a search for meaning' to take place (Bryden 2005, p.162). R2's mouthing of the words of the carol, 'Away in a manger', despite appearing to be asleep, seemed to indicate that something of a spiritual as well as a physical awakening was taking place. It was as though R2 was becoming reacquainted with God's presence in this unknown country.

But this moment of revelation was framed by the anger of his wife, born out of one frustration after another, anger at his present deteriorating condition and anger at her inability to do anything to help. Even if, as Bryden was able to do, the dementia sufferer can view their condition as a voyage of discovery, for their loved ones dementia seems more like a vehicle that is out of control rushing headlong towards certain destruction. And yet, when R2 died, his wife wanted his funeral to be a Christian service, perhaps a recognition 'that there is something within men and women which hints at or speaks of, that which is beyond them' (Goldsmith 2004, p.143).

Conclusion

At the heart of this chapter has been the process of engaging in 'critical dialogue' between the 'contemporary experience' articulated in the seven case studies (encompassing end-of-life care, bereavement, loss (suffered by individuals and groups), disablement and dementia); and the traditional 'norms' from healthcare literature (which range from the psychological, through the clinical to the philosophical and theological). We have also been reflecting upon whether the literature offers any illumination to the case studies which describe what appears to be at first debilitating and disabling chaos. The keeping alive of hope with the possibility of transformation, the adherence to a faith, the communal marking of significant events, giving permission for people to be and become themselves, all of which takes place within loving relationships mirroring the unconditional love God has for his people, points to the enfleshing of God in situations of brokenness and weakness.

3

LISTENING TO THE VOICE OF HISTORICAL EXPERIENCE

Classical Music Born Out of War and Social Fragmentation

Whilst this chapter also continues the process of engaging in 'critical dialogue between theological norms and contemporary experience' (Pattison and Lynch 2005, pp.410–11), in addition, it looks at the language that people use to communicate the presence or absence of God in situations of war and social fragmentation (reflecting some of those experiences already considered). Because so often this communication takes the form of symbol and metaphor, my suggestion is that this process is viewed through the prism of music, its use as a dialogue partner reflecting the 'interdisciplinary approach', which Pattison and Lynch believe is integral to any practical theological research (pp.410–11). Arising out of his work on dementia, Goldsmith reminds us that for some, 'Words can be confusing. Words relating to religion can be even more confusing, and words relating to religious experience can be the most confusing of all' (2004, p.143). Rather than seeing this as a problem, he regards this as an opportunity for new insights, new understanding. It leads him on to suggest that there needs to be an openness to using non-verbal as well as verbal communication that reaches out to a person's inner being and the patience to explore 'what it is that brings solace, satisfaction, hope or meaning to people', what it is that enables their 'being' to have a sense of 'wellbeing' (pp.143–4).

Darkness

To see whether music can indeed provide a meaningful language through which people can communicate the presence or absence of God, I shall consider five musical compositions, each of which, either by virtue of where they were composed and first performed or through the compositions themselves, juxtapose received tradition alongside lived experience. By engaging in critical dialogue and theological reflection, they generate new insights concerning both (after Pattison and Lynch 2005, pp.412, 415–18). The reason for choosing these particular pieces is that each was either written during or addresses issues arising out of periods of war or social fragmentation. These are:

> *Quartet for the End of Time* (*Quatuor pour la fin du temps*) by the French composer Olivier Messiaen (1908–1992), who was himself interned in a POW camp during part of the Second World War.

> *A Child of Our Time* by the English composer Michael Tippett (1905–1998), who was interned in England during part of the Second World War for being a pacifist, this composition being written in response to 'a 17 year old Jewish Jewish boy, Herschel Grynspan' killing a German diplomat in Paris in 1938, an event to which the Nazis' response was Kristallnacht (Tippett 1991, p.39).

> *War Requiem* by the English composer Benjamin Britten (1913–1976), which was commissioned to mark the opening of the new Anglican Cathedral of St Michael and All Angels in Coventry, the first having been destroyed by enemy bombing.

> *Collage: In Memoriam Charles Ives* was composed by me (b.1952) in 1973 in preparation for marking the one-hundredth anniversary since the birth (and twentieth anniversary since the death) of the American composer Charles Ives (1874–1954).

> *Space for Peace* by the priest composer June Boyce-Tillman (b.1943) composed for and first performed on the eve of Holocaust Memorial Day 2009 in Winchester Cathedral and which has subsequently been performed on this day (27 January) and at this venue every year.

In compositions such as these, as well as celebrating (and increasingly nowadays being horrified at) what is, and remembering what has been, composers, as indeed artists in general, are faced with two fundamental questions:

1. Is the artist's function simply to hold up a mirror to the world, acknowledge the suffering that they are witnessing, and reflect what he or she sees?

2. Is the artist's role to encourage, to find a way of surviving the horrors that they are witnessing, and offer hope to a troubled world?

Pope John Paul II (1920–2005) believed that it is the artist's vocation to:

> search for new 'epiphanies' of beauty so that through their creative work as artists, they may offer these as gifts to the world… Even when they explore the darkest depths of the soul or the most unsettling aspects of evil, artists give voice in a way to the universal desire for redemption. (John Paul II 1999, cited in MacMillan 2008, p.12)

James MacMillan (b.1959), a composer himself, believes that art can become 'the bridge that will heal the wound of division' as part of this redemptive process (p.12). If the language of metaphor in art can offer a way of communicating humankind's deepest joys as well as its deepest sorrows, perhaps art can be of help in offering pastoral care a model of discerning, communicating and moving through experiences of acute darkness.

Music both arises out of and returns to silence. Just as 'silence is not of itself neutral', neither is sound; both can be perceived as being oppressive or liberating, God-denying or God-affirming (Winkett 2010, p.136). To know what kind of sound or silence one is being presented with requires discernment on behalf of the listener, whether they also are the initiator of the sound or silence, or not. In this regard, it shows a marked similarity with the listening and discernment that lies at the heart of pastoral care. It is to the role of artist as reflector that I now turn.

Suffering: The artist as a reflector of the suffering that they are witnessing

In his foreword to Winkett's book *Our Sound is Our Wound*, Rowan Williams, in describing her perception of the relationship between beauty and the fallen world, says, 'If we are making perfectly harmonious sounds...something is wrong' (Williams, in Winkett 2010, p.x). As Winkett herself points out, if we are to live authentically within the world, 'the sounds we make...start to reveal deeper theological questions about who we are, of what we are afraid and in whom we trust' (p.3). She relates to the biblical tradition of lament which she describes as 'both a protest against the pain of the present time and also a timeless expression of the weeping voice of God in whose image and likeness we are made' (p.38). It is because she believes that 'the sound is an audible scar of damaged tissue underneath', the sounds we make (and presumably the sound we choose not to make), whether we use words or we choose not to, can be a window into, and a metaphor of, that which lies deep within us, rooted in our individual and collective past, propelling us ever onward, hence the title of her book (p.5). The American theologian Mary McClintock Fulkerson believes that 'creative thinking originates at the scene of a wound. Wounds generate new thinking. Disjunctions birth invention... Like a wound, theological thinking is generated by a sometimes inchoate sense that something *must* be addressed' (2007, pp.13–14). Thus Fulkerson sees responding to a wound as a metaphor for theological thinking itself.

In music, this wound is represented as dissonance. It is dissonance that gives music its tension, the resolving of and discovering of new dissonance that gives it its momentum. That which is regarded as consonance and dissonance, and the degree to which either is in the ascendency, changes with successive generations. Sometimes it is forces external to music that precipitate this change. For example, 'After Auschwitz, it is not appropriate that before God, every cadence resolves, or that every rhythm is comforting' (Winkett 2010, p.34). But even then, a new song emerges; music is still possible. Boyce-Tillman firmly believes that 'inside all of us, there is a musician trying to get out. That musician is our own healer and potentially, through us, the healer of others' (Boyce-Tillman 2000, p.282). In addressing the issue of the painfulness and woundedness of humanity, she believes that 'Pain can be regarded as cracks in a fabric that needs a right relatedness... The disjunctions are the wounds – personal, cultural and cosmic... The music produced is a record of the process of healing.'

Not only can music offer a reflection of the disjointed world in which we live, entering into music making 'offers the possibility of transformed and strengthened living' (p.282). If responding to a wound is also a metaphor for music making, perhaps the making of music offers another way of thinking theologically. I will pursue this suggestion by examining my five chosen works in greater detail to see whether this analogy between doing theology and making music can be substantiated.

In Tippett's *A Child of Our Time*, the sense of woundedness is most readily to be found in the setting of the spirituals. The spirituals provide Tippett with a central point of melodic construction, namely the interval of a minor third (see bracketed material below), which Bowen describes as being 'produced so characteristically in the melodies of the spirituals when moving from the fifth of the tonic to the flat seventh' (Bowen 1982, p.44).

Musical quotation 3.1 Child of Our Time
Extract from second spiritual 'Nobody knows', first four bars, Tenor solo

The playing around with the sighing nature of this unresolved angst inherent in this flattened seventh interval, so crucial in jazz, seems to root this whole work in the collective wound felt by any oppressed peoples. Yet, interestingly, singing with a consonant as well as a dissonant voice at times has appeared problematical. Lucy Winkett reminds us that one of the perceived difficulties with jazz was that 'the same person would sing about faith in God and their experience of the world' (2010, p.78). But, in fact, it is this dichotomy that becomes the musical wound, 'wherein lies the jewel of great price' out of which new life springs (Tippett 2007, p.111)

Tippett's work in general is concerned with woundedness in his portrayal of the 'nameless' perennial 'scapegoat' (Bowen 1982, p.43). Yet within its three parts there is 'a pattern of movement that takes us from the general to the particular and back again' (p.47). It is only in the middle section, for example, that the four soloists are named – soprano, the mother; tenor, the boy; alto, the aunt; and bass, the uncle; some choruses have names too, such as 'Double Chorus of Persecutors and Persecuted' (Tippett 2007, pp.68–71, 59). Furthermore, during the course of the work there is the feeling of movement from winter to spring, from woundedness to healing. The opening chorus begins with the words 'The world turns on its dark side. It is winter.' Part III opens with 'The world descends into the icy waters', but significantly continues, 'Wherein lies the jewel of great price' – foreshadowing the new life which is to come. That would seem to be confirmed by the melismatic setting of choral writing (pp.110–11). Before the penultimate 'Ahs' which lead into the final spiritual, the choir sings 'It is spring' (after Wilfred Owen's poem 'The Seed' (Bowen 1982, p.48)) (Tippett 2007, pp.4–9, 145). Yet one gets the feeling that this journey from winter to summer is not linear but cyclical, the rhythm of nature providing a metaphor for humanity's fragmentation and reconciliation and fragmentation.

For Bowen, 'the main theme of the oratorio' is first articulated in the sixth movement, the tenor solo, the central section of which, during which the voice sings, is set to a tango dance rhythm (Tippett 2007, p.35)! Here Jung's influence can be seen, as it portrays 'the psychologically divided Man, at odds with his Shadow' (Bowen 1982, p.48). Tippett himself describes this central theme in which 'The man tells of his psychological split self which appears to him and actually is on a certain plane the frustrations of his condition in the commonwealth. He has lost the relation to his soul' (Bowen 1980, pp.138–9, cited in Bowen 1982, p.48). The anger that this causes is projected on to others, hence the concept of the scapegoat. As Bowen points out, this divided self only finds any sense of resolution in the penultimate movement, number 29 (Tippett 2007, p.136), 'where it is clearly and movingly encapsulated: "I would know my shadow and my light/so I shall be whole"' (Bowen 1982, p.48). And then follows the affirmation of integration and new life proclaimed in the final spiritual. Or does it? The final spiritual, 'Deep River', ends in a musically unresolved way, again with a sighing minor third (see bracketed material below). Perhaps there simply is no answer to the issues Tippett is exploring.

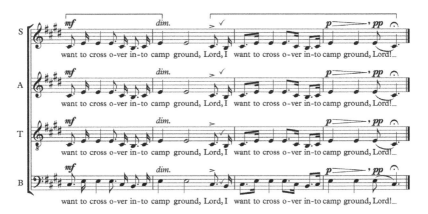

Musical quotation 3.2 A Child of Our Time
Extract from final spiritual 'Deep river', choir part, last four bars of cantata

For other composers, melodic 'woundedness' is portrayed through the interval of the tritone (see bracketed material below).

Musical quotation 3.3 Quatuor pour la fin du temps
Extract from Movement 6 'Danse de la fureur', first two bars

This interval, because of its harmonic ambiguity and its difficulty in being able to be resolved satisfactorily, became known as the 'devil in music' (see bracketed material below). Being neither the interval of a perfect fourth or perfect fifth, but halfway between the two, it screams out against the tonal system in Western music, based as it is upon the cycle of rising fifths for sharp keys and falling fifths for flat keys. In Messiaen's *Quatuor pour la fin du temps*, this device is one of the ways he contrasts what *is* from what *will be*.

Thus in 'Abîme des oiseaux' (Movement 3), written for unaccompanied clarinet, which is a movement full of contrast between slow and fast, sad and fun-filled, very soft growing in dynamics to very loud within a single bar (Messiaen 1941, bars 13 and 21, p.15), and in which echo effects, within widely and closely spaced melodic material, are much used; the interval of the tritone features repeatedly. In 'Danse de la fureur, pour les sept trompettes' (Movement 6), which is one of four movements to use all four instrumentalists (although not all play all the time), and which 'stands apart in that the instruments play in unison or octaves throughout' is another movement full of contrasts (pp.23–5). It has a breathless quality and is extremely exciting, employing as it does an 'ametric' (irregular) style of rhythmic writing, the metrical equivalent of woundedness, with much of it being loud and extremely fast.

Musical quotation 3.4 Quatuor pour la fin du temps
Extract from Movement 6 'Danse de la fureur', first six bars, violin part

These sections are set alongside less hectic sections. Again there is a feeling that the tritone predominates (most particularly between F# and C), representing opposite tonal polarities (compare Messiaen 1941, bars 1–4, with bars 5–8, pp.23–4, letter D–E, pp.25–6 and subsequent similar places).

But perhaps the most striking use of the tritone as musical wound occurs in Britten's *War Requiem* (see bracketed material below).

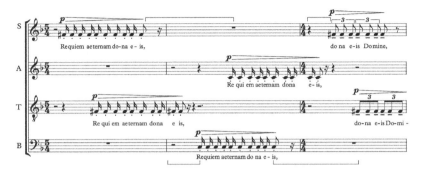

Musical quotation 3.5 War Requiem
Extract from 'Requiem Aeternam', choir part, first four bars

One of the great ironies of the *War Requiem* is that the tritone is employed as a principal force for unity within it. Yet in this work, the 'un-peaceful' tritone interval of F# and C natural 'always appears in relation to the idea of "requiem"' (Evans 1979, p.452).

It is the opening interval sung by the choir at the beginning of the first movement, 'Requiem aeternam'. It straddles the boys' material 'Te decet hymnus Deus in Sion' and exists between the harp accompaniment and tenor solo in the passage beginning 'what passing bells'. It is in the closing tubular bell notes and dominates the concluding choral writing of the same movement (and that of the 'Dies Irae' (Movement 2) and the 'Libera Me' (Movement 6)) before the unaccompanied choir's magical resolution into F major (Britten 1997, pp.1–2, 8–9, 16, 24, 90, 238). It is present in the choice of tonal centres in the 'Offertorium' (Movement 3), vacillating between the C# minor of the boys' opening material and the G major of the choral fugue (pp.91, 97). It pervades the 'Sanctus' (Movement 4) in the opening percussion, soprano solo and chorus 'fluttering' material (the latter of which equally well conjures up the Tower of Babel as Pentecost, depending upon one's own perspective of things), before the grandiose D major orchestral material (pp.140–4, 145–51).

But does the 'requiem' material provide a real resolution at the end of movements 1, 2 and 6 or not? Evans suggests that 'this cannot be regarded as "the outcome" in the long term (or even notably logical) sense of each of the three movements that cadence in this way' (Evans 1979, p.452). It is in the shortest movement of the *War Requiem*, the 'Agnus Dei' (Movement 6; just eight pages in the full score), that resolution is finally achieved.

In this movement, the tritone interval provides the twin points of reference in the ascending and descending semi-quavers that variously pervade the choral and orchestral writing and the tenor solo especially pp.170–1 and pp.175–8 (Britten 1997, pp.170–8; see bracketed material below). Again the metrical equivalent of a wound, an irregular time signature (that of five semiquavers to a bar; see 3.6) also emphasizes an initial feeling of dislocation, similar to the way in which the irregular time signature (that of seven crotchets to a bar; see 3.7) emphasizes an initial feeling of dislocation at certain points within the 'Dies Irae' (pp.25, 27, 30, 33, 72).

Musical quotation 3.6 War Requiem
Extract from 'Agnus Dei', first four bars

Musical quotation 3.7 War Requiem
Extract from 'Dies Irae', bars 2–5, piano, choir, strings

Evans is of the opinion that despite its brevity, 'only the Agnus Dei achieves a final statement of an equipoise in which the strains of the whole movement are balanced out' (1979, p.452). This is underscored by a coming together of the music to which Wilfred Owen's poetry and the 'Agnus Dei' is set and the sentiments of the words themselves, 'between Owen's salutation of the "greater love", and the liturgy's prayers for "requiem sempiternam" reinforced by the addition of the words by Britten "Dona nobis pacem" in the tenor's cadential phrase' (p.452). So, not only at the centre of this movement, but at the centre of this composition, it is a musical 'wound', the tritone, that is used as a force for reconciliation.

The general sense of woundedness which permeates the whole of *Collage*, as with the *War Requiem*, is that caused by my desire for *Collage* to set text which proclaimed the presence of God alongside text which proclaimed God's absence (see Appendix 2). Being written in memory of the composer Charles Ives, and as a feature of Ives' writing was to juxtapose disparate musical strands alongside one another, strands that could even be in different keys or in different time signatures (reputedly influenced by listening to approaching and departing marching bands of his youth), the driving force behind *Collage* is the contrast set up between these two types of text and the musical material that accompanies them. Ives-like, it asks 'the un-answered question' 'Why?'

In the musical material used, there is a contrast between the orchestral diatonic 'love' theme (with which the composition begins and ends; see 3.8), and the atonal choral music which accompanies the words concerned with lovelessness from 1 Corinthians 13 (3.9). The diatonic material is also picked up by a jazzy setting of 1 Corinthians 13, words describing childish imperfect knowledge. Angular atonal material is used also to set the tomorrow and tomorrow; speech as it is to set the words describing drug withdrawal. Lack of tonality is used to represent lack of love. Rhythmically, there is a recurring insistent figure that is both a source of unity in the work and symbolizes the 'Why?' question that simply will not go away (3.10). And all the while, liturgical music recurs in the background with no engagement in the main thematic or rhythmic material symbolising a lack of engagement with the traditional Church in lived experience.

Collage uses differently constituted groups of musicians spaced around the audience, the different groups either being assigned different texts or remaining text-less. In addition to the live musicians, there are the three pieces of pre-recorded material for organ and choir (played through three separate speakers positioned spatially around the audience) which are settings of Ralph Vaughan Williams' (1872–1958) 'Psalm 150', John Merbecke's (1510–1585) 'Glory be to God on high' and the hymn 'God moves in a mysterious way'. The climax of the work is when the lines 'God is his own interpreter, and he will make it plain' are heard in isolation, followed by strident trombones and full organ. This in turn gives way to the return of the opening choral setting of 1 Corinthians 13 and the 'love' music. Is life 'a tale told by an idiot full of sound and fury signifying nothing', or is it the greatest gift that God can give us? Are the different voices we hear throughout our human existence signs of chaos and fragmentation or signs of the rich variety of life in all its fullness and its possibility for healing and integration? Are they symbols of Babel or Pentecost? As the audience hears the various texts, the hope is that new meanings are generated through their various juxtapositions. Thus the question is not just 'Why do we live?' but 'How will God give us any idea as to why he has called us into being?' As was noticed with Tippett and Britten, the answer would seem to have to have something to do with love.

Musical quotation 3.8 Collage
Extract from the love theme, bars 17–23, string parts

Musical quotation 3.9 Collage
Extract from the atonal material, bars 85–93, voice parts

Musical quotation 3.10 Collage
Extract from the repeated rhythmic pattern, bars 92–96

Music seems to lend itself to the holding together of opposites. June Boyce-Tillman believes that one of the insights of music therapy has meant that 'the process of integration can be seen as the state of the peaceful co-existence of diversity which can be encouraged musically by the use of diverse motifs and instruments' (2000, p.245). Or put slightly differently, 'Music, unlike any other art or discipline, requires the ability to express oneself with absolute commitment and passion whilst listening carefully and sensitively to another voice which may even contradict one's own statement' (Barenboim 2008, cited in Winkett 2010, p.77). But health and healing may not just be found through integration and within what one finds comfortable, but by pushing against that which one finds comfortable in order to explore pastures new (Boyce-Tillman 2000, p.14). Health, as life, she regards as a dynamic process, and thus eminently suitable to be symbolized by the dynamic art of music where adults as well as children can learn to play once again (p.19).

Surviving: The artist as a beacon of hope and a means of survival

Music, when performed, in a very real sense exists in the present moment. It continually comes alive in each successive present moment. Because of its existing within a single moment and within time generally, the theologian Jeremy Begbie sees music as '*enacting theological wisdom*', a wisdom that is already in existence because God is already in existence (2000, p.5). He agrees with Rowan Williams that 'What we learn, in music as in the contemplative faith of which music is a part and also a symbol, is what it is to work *with* the [temporal] grain of things, to work in the stream of God's wisdom' (Williams 1994, cited in Begbie 2000, p.97). Because of its use of 'delay and patience' and 'promise and fulfillment', music is a symbol for the finite *doing* world held as it is within the infinity of God's *being* world (p.127). It is not surprising, therefore, that music is one of the vehicles favoured for worshipping God.

In dedicating *Quatuor pour la fin du temps* 'In homage to the Angel of the Apocalypse who lifts his hand towards the heavens and says: "There will be no more time"' (Messiaen 1941), Olivier Messiaen could be understood as joining in with what Winkett describes as the music of the angels, music which takes the form of a 'kind of thunderous gentle melody that leaves you struggling to breathe because it has revealed the truth in an instant about love and beauty, loss and revelation' (Winkett 2010, pp.103, 114).

In 'Louange à l'Éternité de Jésus' (Movement 5), the slow cello parts combined with the repeated chordal writing of the piano part, serves to generate a timeless quality to the piece. The soft cello harmonics at letter D add to its ethereal nature (Messiaen 1941, p.22). In 'Louange à l'Immortalité de Jésus' (Movement 8), the lyrical violin part, for the most part employing triplet rhythm, contrasted with the throbbing piano part, dominated by second inversion E major harmony, again produces a feeling of timelessness. The low sonority to the piano notes (bottom of p.50 to top of p.52) contrasted with the very high violin writing at the end of the movement adds to this feeling of space. In 'Vocalise pour l'Ange qui annonce la fin du Temps' (Movement 2), the dropping out of the clarinet part after just two pages, and the slower tempo, leaves the unison strings ethereally playing 'ond martineau-like' above repeated piano chords, suggesting once again a feeling of timelessness.

Rather than focusing on the suffering of the times in which he is living, Messiaen chooses to focus on the majesty of God and the eternal dimension in which our transitory world is set. Messiaen makes clear 'that this quartet was written for the end of time, not as a play on words about the time of captivity, but for the ending of concepts of past and future: that is, for the beginning of eternity' (Golea 1960, p.64, cited in Pople 1998, p.13).

Messiaen is not the only composer to compose whilst being incarcerated during the Second World War. Pople draws attention to those who produced music at Theresienstadt, 'a staging post on their journey to the gas chambers' (1998, p.14). Those who compose in such difficult circumstances:

> more than bear comparison with Messiaen as a victory through art of humanity over inhumanity… Whereas they knew for certain they were living on borrowed time…Messiaen was driven to contemplate time in quite a different way, focusing on theological truths about the end of *all* time. (p.14)

Messiaen's great message of hope is to remind a humanity imprisoned in time that temporality is itself located within an eternal reality.

For Boyce-Tillman, the offering of hope to a troubled world is not to be found by looking ahead to the end of time, but the looking back beyond particularism and to universalism, to that original goodness inherent within each individual, agreeing with Gill that 'Incompatible…movements' within as well as between faiths 'need… enlightenment, the whole necessarily being greater than the sum of the parts' (Gill 2010, p.416). Her *Space for Peace* is tapping into to the 'divine harmony' of which Maurice speaks, 'a divine harmony, of which the living principle in each of these systems forms one note, of which the systems themselves are a disturbance and violation' (Maurice 1837, p.308, cited in Gill 2010, p.418).

June Boyce-Tillman's search for peace is set against the backdrop of genocidal horrors. With the exception of the first performance, the subsequent performances have all begun with a short act of remembrance with prayers said and candles lit by representatives of the three monotheistic faiths, Jew, Christian and Muslim, after a moment of silence has been kept. Boyce-Tillman describes this composition as being 'an exciting way to explore a new way of music and meditation'. It is 'a musical vigil for peace' (Boyce-Tillman 2011, p.1). In this composition, each group brings to the performance items that it wishes to perform. These are combined with chants which the composer has written (which themselves seem to arise out of the initial traditional 'Shalom' tune with its accompanying text), the juxtaposition of difference and sameness, variety and unity, present experience set alongside a future hope being a central concept of this work.

Musical quotation 3.11 Space for Peace
Traditional chant (Shalom salaam…), bars 9–17, congregational part

Because every time the work is performed, different groups will bring a different selection of music to sing or to play, and these will interact with other groups' music in different ways, this composition can never be performed again in the same way. It exists in time for a moment, and then is gone. Thus the composer is not a mere writer of notes, but a facilitator and enabler of the music making of others, a provider of 'space' in which 'peace' can be experienced. The composer as facilitator and enabler is an intentional approach on Boyce-Tillman's part as she believes that lasting peace can only be created from the 'bottom up', as the 'top down' method so easily becomes one individual or group exerting power over another, which has been tried in the past and found wanting.

The first and last sections of *Space for Peace* consist of seven folk-like themes in D minor, which, as they are piled one upon the other, again create a sense of either Babel or Pentecost. Over time, there is a sense in which, because the semitones and tones lose their distinctiveness, melodic individuality disappears; and because different chords lose their distinctiveness and harmonic movement stops, a musical language becomes established in which everything appears to harmonize with everything else. This is not surprising as the initial traditional tune, with which the work both begins and ends, is itself a four-part round. The Babel of division gives way to the Pentecost of peace.

She believes that music can indeed be used as force for reconciliation as it can symbolize healing and wholeness by stressing the importance of inter- and intra-connectedness, 'within the body, human being to human being, humans to the natural world, human beings and the natural world to God or the spiritual' (Boyce-Tillman

2000, p.10). This view of music, which stresses the intuitive over the rational, stands counter to the prevailing 'Western post-Enlightenment culture' in which the reverse is the case (p.10). She believes that a balance needs to be struck between these two types of knowledge, as she maintains that 'All ways of knowing lie within each individual… they can be validated through music-making.' So '[m]usic making potentially becomes a way of challenging the dominant value system, as well also of supporting it' (p.13). Thus Boyce-Tillman encourages us to discover, or rediscover, our own unique voice.

The chaplain as reflector and as a beacon of hope

This chapter has explored the use of music as a language that can be used to communicate God's presence or absence in various dark experiences. It has looked specifically at whether the artist's function is simply to hold up a mirror to the woundedness of the world and reflect what he or she sees, or to offer hope by discerning the infinite breaking in upon a finite troubled world. Within the hospital setting, the chaplain, in listening to the stories people 'sing' both in isolation from and in communion with other 'singers, has the dual role (reflecting the two points above) which Winkett sees as falling to the wider Church. First, in 'holding up a microphone to the patient's world view and replay(ing) what he or she hears', the chaplain can act as 'critical friend' (2010, p.131). Second, in seeking 'to offer hope to' persons caught up within 'a troubled world', the chaplain can help them to find their authentic voice, by calling 'people into silence in the presence of God' (p.134).

Conclusion

The search for God (holding up a mirror to the world and reflecting what is seen), and the God for whom one searches (the offering of hope to a troubled world), seems full of dialectical imagery of darkness and light in persistent *collage* (Fulkerson 2007, pp.13–14). Both seem characterized by antimony which 'simultaneously admits the truth of two contradictions, logically incompatible, ontologically equally necessary assertions' and which 'testifies to the existence of a mystery beyond which human reason cannot penetrate' (Bulgakov 1937, p.116, cited in Garrison 1982, p.27). Each of the works considered above, either through where they were composed and first performed or through the compositions themselves, juxtapose received tradition alongside lived experience. Messiaen sought to place his concentration camp experience within an eternal perspective. Tippett and Britten demanded some kind of response from received traditions when faced with the horrors of war. My piece looks for a meaning beyond the statement of opposites. Boyce-Tillman searches for unity in diversity. If 'theological thinking is generated by a sometimes inchoate sense that something *must* be addressed' (Fulkerson 2007, pp.13–14), as Garrison has said of philosophy and theology, so, I believe, the same can be said of music and theology, that 'both...cohere in a living dynamic relationship, keeping their respective identities, and yet producing a synthesis greater that either of their parts' (1982, p.59). It is therefore possible that the way that music functions helps us better understand how practical theology functions, especially as it finds expression through the medium of pastoral care.

4

LISTENING TO THE VOICE OF PASTORAL EXPERIENCE

(1) Classical Music as a Means of Discerning Sameness and Difference

This chapter continues to employ music as a dialogue partner reflecting an 'interdisciplinary approach', as it explores whether contrasting musical polarities and/or musical form can in any way inform and enlighten pastoral care. The juxtaposition of disparate elements would seem to be at the centre of all music in general, and Western music in particular. At heart, this manifests itself between sameness and difference. The musical polarities I am suggesting using here are not as complex or inter-related as the seven musical polarities employed by June Boyce-Tillman, which she sees as 'mirror(ing) the process of living and which can be related to the nature of music' and which she sees as representing 'continuums within the self' (2000, pp.4–32). I am suggesting looking at how sameness and difference manifests itself in music in the following ways:

a. sound and silence (music making), high and low (pitch), pulse and rhythm (tempo), loud and soft (dynamics), unison and harmony (harmonic language), and musical colour (timbre)

b. new and repeated musical material (musical form).

As well as noting in passing how the relationship within these pairings and between these categories changes with the passing of time, and how this may also throw light upon the changing relationship between systematic and practical theology, my main concern here is to explore, through reference to the seven case studies considered earlier, whether a better discernment of sameness and difference may have something helpful to say about what is being voiced (or remaining unvoiced) within the pastoral encounter.

Contrasting musical polarities

Sound and silence

Sound forms part of a continuum of vibrating frequencies, only part of which can be sensed by us. These frequencies are variously perceived as rhythm, pitch and light. Within the auditory frequency range, the most elementary contrast between sameness and difference occurs when one is deciding whether to make a sound or not make one. Because the natural world is full of all kinds of sounds, our ancestors would not have had the experience of total silence, not even in the middle of the night. So their choice would have been to join in or not join with the sounds taking place all around them. As well as being objective and observable (albeit aurally), sound and silence can mean different things to different people. Both can represent positive or negative qualities, be wanted or unwanted. Sound can represent life in all its fullness or chaotic cacophony; silence can represent death or it can represent the stillness that comes before new birth.

For example, the quaver rest with which the first movement of Beethoven's Fifth Symphony begins is the springboard from which that symphony is launched.

In the early days of human civilization, all music would have been considered religious in that it was responding to something beyond the individual and even a community of individuals. Joining in with these pre-existing sounds may well have come about as one way of responding to the world in which human beings found themselves and of the creative force behind it, and as a way of individuals and groups asserting their own particular identity. In the former can be found the origins of religious music, and in the latter of secular music. This division seems to have become more pronounced as human beings began to cease working directly on the land and to move away from the countryside, and in doing so, lose touch with it and settle in conurbations.

Individual sounds, as with all that lives within the natural world, are born, have duration and die. An obvious way of beginning this process would be to copy the sounds that are already being heard, the sounds of the birds, the wild animals, a storm, the sea, one another.

Composers have continued to do this down through the centuries, two more recent example being Respighi's *The Birds* and Debussy's *La Mer*.

But there are also sounds within, and generated by, the human person too: the heart beat and pulse, the breathing in and out, walking, skipping and dancing, Having begun the process by copying what is heard, it then becomes possible to play around with these sounds, to change them, to make them one's own, to recreate them, to compose new sounds. The reproduction of these sounds and their incorporation within music making would not have happened in isolation from other activities. As one sees in tribal communities today that still maintain their contact with the land, music, dance and religious ritual are intimately bound up one with another.

REFLECTION – HELPING A PERSON DECIDE WHETHER OR NOT TO SPEAK

Within the pastoral encounter, a decision has to be made as to whether to talk or to stay silent. Space has to be given for both; as has already been observed, both are capable of positive and negative communication. It may be that sound is not initially the primary source of communication, in which case all the senses of the pastoral carer need to be attuned to what is or is not taking place. An example of this discernment is suggested by Pattison when he urges an awareness of people's secular and religious artefacts and the importance they attach to them (2007, pp.6–14). Once a person's story begins to unfold, it may copy other narratives or violently react against them (such as narratives of faith). In time, a person may discover their own unique voice.

High and low

The exploring of singing differing pitches may have started with the singing of a single note, reacting and responding to one's situation, or it may have come about by copying a sound directly from nature.

The cuckoo is an obvious example, employing as it does the fall of a minor third. In listening to children playing across the world, in their singing games this interval is likely to feature, but developed so that after the fall of the minor third there is the rise of a fourth, followed by the drop of a tone and the falling minor third again. The singing of this pattern is so deeply engrained across the world that it suggests a collective musical sub-conscious. Furthermore, when sung in compound time, it lends itself not just to play but to work requiring repetitive action.

In the hospital in which I used to work, the sound of the falling minor lives on in the cry of the 'bun man', who brings sandwiches and other delicacies (including buns) to staff in offices and on the wards. The cry of the 'bun run' brings staff and the more mobile of patients to ward entrances to sample his wares.

Whether one starts with a single note or with a falling minor third, the natural way to begin to explore pitch is by step, rising and falling. In the Gregorian plainsong music of the early Church (dating from the second half of the sixth century), this is exactly what happens: it uses non-stepwise movement to mark an ending or a beginning. Over time, these patterns of rising and falling notes acquired a focal note, different focal notes giving a different feel to the pattern of notes based around it. These evolved into modes, each mode being named after a different Greek tribe. The modal system is perhaps best understood in terms of using all the white notes on the piano, each mode having a different white note as it focal note.

The modal system was just one way of organizing patterns of differing pitches. Another way came about when two modes themselves assumed an importance over and above the other modes. These became the major and minor keys upon which the majority of Western music has been and continues to be primarily based. Keys having different focal notes require the same pattern of tones and semitones to be replicated. The key system is perhaps best understood in terms of being able to use the white and the black notes on the piano, each key having a different white or black note as it focal note.

A further way of organizing pitch patterns, known as serial (or atonal) music, is that advocated by Arnold Schoenberg and the Second Viennese School at the beginning of the twentieth century in which all 12 semitones are considered as being of equal importance, thus emulating a kind of musical democracy. (Some serial pieces apply this disciplined democracy to rhythm as well.) Any note can become a focal note. Any note can be combined with any other note. Scales have been replaced by series or (tone rows) from which this music gets its name. Its discipline comes from the fact that in the tone row on which the music is based all 12 notes have to occur once. That which gives the tone row its character is the order and pitch in which these notes occur. *Collage*, one of the compositions considered above in Chapter 3, employs serialism through part of its construction.

REFLECTION – HELPING A PERSON DISCOVER THEIR OWN UNIQUE VOICE

In the first case study, T's response to his illness cannot fail to be affected by the fact that before his diagnosis he was an extremely active person who used the very active sport of football to provide youngsters with a positive influence in their lives. His story (which is how he reacts to his illness) begins with his diagnosis and will end in a very real sense when he is no longer able to talk (although there is a sense of it ending at the moment his funeral eulogy has ended). His twin focal points appear to be his family (and friends) and his refusal to give up. His story struggles to assert T the man over and above T the terminally ill patient.

In the second case study, C's parents are initially responding to the death of their little girl. But they are also responding to the unfairness of her terminal diagnosis in a child so young, compounded by the fact that there were a number of other children who lived locally who all had been diagnosed with a terminal illness. This unfairness very quickly turned to anger, more openly voiced by C's father than her mother, which became a real focus in their grieving. Over time, with outside facilitation, this anger, whilst it did not totally disappear, was replaced by a sense of celebrating the lives of all children in the locality who had died as a result of terminal illness.

In the third case study, S is responding to the fact that what should have been a very straightforward procedure could have gone so terribly wrong. She too is angered by the unfairness of things, and this within the context of an active Christian faith which she feels should make her more accepting of things. A major focus for her during her illness is her strong sense of body image. When she is faced with the stark decision of amputation or death, her initial decision not to go ahead with the amputation is very much out of tune with her doctors and members of her family.

In the fourth case study, it is unclear what precipitated the psychotic incident which led to A being admitted into hospital. Whatever it was, it manifested itself in a chaotic state and a confusion with boundaries. She longed for a sense of order in her life, which she seemed to find in biblical narrative stories concerned with wilderness and sanctuary, and the regular reception of Holy Communion. Sadly, one feels that her chaotic story will never end, as she remains out of tune with those around her.

In the fifth case study, the staff are reacting to their hitherto world of stability being thrown into a state of flux twice. Whilst it is clear that the beginning of their story coincides with the beginning of them coming together as a team, it has ended in a state of fragmentation. Their story has become focused in a perceived sense of management betrayal. This seems to have been fed by the management's inability to discern what the staff were feeling, which was an acute sense of grief, with something precious having 'died', and with no body to mourn.

In the sixth case study, the staff are reacting not only to the death of R1 but also to what his death represents for the residential accommodation in which he lives and in which they work. Will the accommodation change its function, will it shut, will they be out of work? In addition, whereas others might note the death of a profoundly handicapped man, they mourn the loss of a much loved member of their community. In preparation for his funeral, it was clear that staff members had become by default R1's substitute family.

In the last case study, the death of R2 is a matter of sadness for the staff, who have come to know him very well since he has been with them, but especially for his wife. Her grief at his dementia and death gives vent to her anger about the way that she (a white European) and he (of Afro-Caribbean descent) have been treated throughout their married life. This sometimes led to outbursts of anger even at the dementia centre where the staff had a real affection for R2, because she found it impossible to process. Life had been and continued to be for her a huge struggle.

Pulse and rhythm

Musical pulse has at its centre that pulse which exists within the human person, which finds expression within the beat of the human heart pumping blood around the body and the filling and emptying of lungs with air which oxygenates this blood. It also finds expression in the human activities of speaking (the words spoken encapsulating their own metre), walking, skipping, dancing and repeated actions of any kind. Musical pulse is thus an affirmation of the life found within the human person and their activities in particular, and the natural world in general. It is not just that musical pulse owes its origins to human pulse, inspiration and exhalation, but the effect that a particular musical pulse has upon us is entirely contingent upon its continued relationship with human pulse, a faster pulse generating excitement, a slower pulse tranquillity.

One of the ironies of musical temporal history is that when regular pulse did become established in church music, a favourite pulse grouping was that of three beats to the bar as a reminder of the three persons of God the Holy Trinity. In a later period, when a faster three beats in a bar became associated with the Viennese waltz, not only would that not have been considered appropriate for use in church, but it took time to be accepted for dancing in polite society because of the perceived close proximity of the dancers with each other.

The pulse of music can be considered its skeleton, but its temporal body is given shape by its rhythm, which is a way of subdividing, or combining, or even deviating from individual pulses in a variety of different ways. Within musical time, there is the constant interplay between the pulse (which itself can be regular or irregular) and rhythm, just as there is between movement and stasis.

REFLECTION – HELPING A PERSON DISCOVER
THEIR OWN UNIQUE PULSE AND RHYTHM OF LIFE

In the first case study, the pulse and rhythm of T's life was greatly disrupted by his diagnosis. His inner pulse leads him to be naturally positive and outgoing, his rhythm of life driving him ever onward to try new things. Once his illness had been diagnosed, there was a sense of there being no time to waste. His determination to walk the Normandy beaches provided an example of his rhythm of life struggling to fight against his deteriorating pulse of life.

In the second case study, again the death of C severely disrupted the family's rhythm of life. It had to discover a new pulse of living, indeed a new reason to live at all. The needs of other family members helped establish this new family pulse. The anger of C's parents and other parents with terminally ill children might best be conveyed as violent syncopations against the pulse of life that only found a kind of tranquillity once the regular children's memorial services became established.

In the third case study, S experienced the infection after her operation as a fracture to her pulse of faith and rhythm of living. That was as nothing to the literal and metaphorical fracture to these precipitated by her amputation. Whilst the nurturing of her faith through the reception of Holy Communion during this period was vital, her perception was that she would never experience tranquillity in her life ever again.

In the fourth case study, A, in the midst of her chaos, became very excited when she was about to receive Holy Communion, and appeared to experience great tranquillity afterwards. Her rhythms of living were at times so disruptive that it proved impossible to discern any undergirding ordered pulse of living at all. Because the beginning of her life story remains unclear, perhaps the best way of understanding her life musically is that of continual syncopation.

In the fifth case study, the staff are thrown from a period of stasis, through two periods of intense movement and disruption to decreasing periods of tranquillity. The pulse of peaceful living is strong for them to begin with. This strong pulse gradually becomes fainter and fainter, with the disruptive rhythms of syncopated frustrated living predominating. The inner pulse of the ward staff is not the same as the inner pulse of the managerial staff, the two appearing to have no relationship one with another.

In the sixth case study, when R1 was alive, despite that which was important in his life being different to many other people's, he demanded that others fell in time with his pulse for living, and many did. Within the tempo of his life, he developed a very happy and fulfilling rhythm. Therefore his death marked a huge interruption to the rhythm of the lives of those who were closest to him which they experienced not as a period of stasis, but as devastating sense of loss.

In the last case study, despite R2 suffering from end-stage dementia, he achieved a huge sense of tranquillity during the final carol service that he attended, the words of 'Away in a manger', in describing events of long ago, unlocking for him memories of long ago. Again his death caused a major disruption in the lives of those closest to him, particularly his wife. As the pulse of her life had for so many years been bound up with the pulse of his life, perhaps unsurprisingly, his death caused her natural rhythm of life to lose any meaningful sense of focus.

Loud and soft

In one sense, the history of the dynamics of Western music can be seen as being much influenced by music moving from being performed outside in the open air to being performed inside a building, mirroring sociologically the change from living and working in the country to living and working in the town. Clearly, this is a gross over-simplification. Music continues to be performed outside not just in open-air concerts but also functionally – for example, in accompanying folk dancing, or as an aid to marching. But the trend it articulates seems to hold true. Whilst voices are just as capable of singing in the open air as indoors, a move from outside to inside could not have happened without an accompanying refinement of tone that came with an evolution in musical instruments.

For example, the rebec was replaced by the viol and later the violin, the shawm was replaced by the oboe, and the sackbut was replaced by the trombone.

The string, woodwind, brass and percussion instruments with which we are now so well accustomed are just as capable of playing loudly as softly. Indeed, varying the dynamics between and within various pieces of music is one of the ways music maintains interest and vibrancy. Varying musical dynamics first happened in blocks of sound, often mirroring different groups of sound generators. It happened in performance before being written down in the music, early Baroque music having no dynamic indicators in the score at all. Getting gradually louder or softer is a relatively late addition in the evolution of dynamics in Western music.

Perhaps the most famous introduction of a gradual crescendo was the 'Manheim Skyrocket', which happened under Karl Stamitz in the eighteenth century. The desire to gradually increase or decrease dynamics was mirrored on the organ by the addition of a swell pedal which can be gradually opened (causing the sound to get louder) or closed (to get softer).

It is perfectly possible, of course, for contrasting dynamics to be happening in music at the same time. Because brass instruments are naturally louder than woodwind instruments which are louder than strings, for the louder instruments to play the same dynamics as the quieter ones, the former may need to be marked quieter than the latter in the score. Similarly, if a solo voice/instrument or vocal/instrumental group is playing at the same time as the main group, the former may need to be marked louder than the latter. This is also true if one part is playing or singing short staccato notes against other parts' smooth legato notes. But the principle use of contrasting dynamics at the same time is when a specific musical effect (which is often also dramatic) is required. For example, in an orchestral piece, strings can be marked softer than brass and wind but carry on playing after the louder instruments have stopped, giving the impression of a wash of sound growing out of the silence.

REFLECTION – HEARING A SINGLE VOICE
AMIDST THE MANY OTHER VOICES

In the first case study, the voice of T was loud and firm until the moment when he could no longer speak at all. The voices of his friends were heard by hospice staff but probably wouldn't have been heard in the same way by hospital staff, and so he could periodically be 'kidnapped' by them. Through his eulogy, his voice was 'heard' at his own funeral which gave the impression that, despite the silencing of that voice by death, in a very real sense, he had the last word.

In the second case study, the voice of C's mother was very much in evidence in the planning of her daughter's funeral. But it was eclipsed by the loud and angry voice of her husband who demanded that his anger be heard. The angry voices of other parents of terminally ill children similarly demanded to be heard but were voiced though the mothers of these children, the fathers either not wanting, or not able, to be present. The silence of the memorial garden is in stark contrast to all of this, being a place where children can come and be quiet and for those who knew C to remember her.

In the third case study, S's voice found it hard to be heard when the matter of whether or not to have one of her legs amputated was being discussed. The medical staff and S's family saw the decision as being very easy to make. It was a decision to live or a decision to die. The certainty of what the right answer was made their voices very loud. S allowed her voice to be silenced for her family's sake. When at the end of her hospital stay she was able to quietly acknowledge that she had made the wrong decision, it mirrored discordant strings left sounding after the brass had ceased.

In the fourth case study, there is a complicated cacophony of voices all demanding to be heard. There was the little girl who loved being read stories but whose childhood ended with abuse. There was the adult woman crying out for help, longing to be loved, finding that the only way she could attract people's attention was to say and do bizarre things. There was the woman of faith whose loud chaotic voices stilled after she had received Holy Communion, but then after a period reasserted themselves again.

In the fifth case study, the voice of healthcare managers shouted louder than the ward staff concerned. Indeed, there seemed to be a failure to hear their voices at all without attention being drawn to them by a third party. From the ward staff's point of view, there seemed to be two voices demanding to be expressed. The louder of these voices was that expressing anger and betrayal and lack of being valued; the softer of these voices was that expressing sadness and grief.

In the sixth case study, the predominant voice being expressed by the staff was that of grief. Despite R1's profound learning disabilities, the love for him was so great that members of staff who had worked with R1 (but were no longer working at the Trust) wanted their feelings of loss articulated loud and clear. There was also an underlying voice that was not being overtly articulated, and that concerned the future of the centre and the future of people's jobs.

In the last case study, again a number of voices were present. First, there was that voice which expressed sorrow that the dementia centre had changed from being a respite centre to an assessment centre. Second, there was an understanding that the Christmas carol service and Christmas party emphasized the personhood of patients over and above their diagnoses. Third, there was the quietness of R2 as he mouthed the words of 'Away in a manger'. Fourth, there was the loudness of R2's widow over multiple frustrations of which his death proved the final straw.

Unison and harmony

In copying the sounds around, the first music makers would have been aware of a distinction between high and low sounds. As well as being present in nature in general, they are specifically present within humankind, between women and children on the one hand, and men on the other. Over time these gradations of pitch generators could be further subdivided until we get close to those voices represented in a conventional choir today. The first adventure in communal singing would have occurred when one person copied what he/she heard another person singing and a relationship between them was established. Perhaps their actually singing together came about by accident, when instead of copying the lead singer, they happened to sing the same music at the same time. If the two people singing are not of the same broad vocal range, one with a high voice and one with a low one, they would not be singing the same notes but notes one/two octaves apart, resulting in unison singing.

Singing together at intervals other than an octave apart may well have come about by two voices starting on the same note, one voice staying on the same note by way of a drone and the other rising and falling by step. Apart from the unison note between two voices and the octave interval between high and low voices (1–8), the next significant intervals would have been the fifth (1–5) and fourth (5–8). Maybe this was because of a fifth's and fourth's 'half way' feeling between the two notes of an octave or because of these being the intervals that naturally separate the pitch of high and low women's and children's voices, and high and low men's voices. Their musical vibrations act together as points of stasis. Their importance can be seen in Gregorian plainsong – for example, by parts moving together in parallel in intervals of a fifth and fourth, known as organum (dating from the ninth century).

In tonal music, the intervals of a fourth, fifth and octave are understood as perfect intervals, incapable of being major or minor intervals, only capable of being augmented or diminished intervals. The tritone (which is an augmented fourth as well as being a diminished fifth) was discussed above in Chapter 3.

In the first of these examples of part singing (where one part acts a drone) can be seen the origins of contrapuntal music; in the second (in which parts move at the same time), homophonic music. In time, as two or more parts began to move independently, as the interval between those parts changed, points of stasis would alternate with points of tension demanding stasis, and the discipline of harmony was born. Different epochs in time would have different views on what constituted tension and stasis, consonance and dissonance.

REFLECTION – HEARING IF A SINGLE VOICE IS IN HARMONY OR IN CONFLICT WITH OTHER VOICES

In the first case study, T's voice throughout his illness remained in harmony with the voices of his family and friends. He refused as far as it was possible to be dominated and subjugated by the voice of his illness. He worked in harmony with the voices of the healthcare professionals; what they were saying inevitably gave a minor flavour to the way he lived his life. His courage in walking the Normandy beaches, whilst not making him a loner, very definitely set him apart from the herd.

The second case study underlines the fact that anyone who experiences the death of a child feels isolated from the surrounding community, as nobody knows what to say. Inadvertently, they can have a sense of 'being sent to Coventry'. C's parents found themselves in harmony with other families with terminally ill children, and out of harmony with some ward and community staff. How could they have let their little girl die? That which ultimately seemed to bring some kind of consonance to this dissonance was the annual memorial service, where their names were remembered.

In the third case study, S's voice is out of harmony with other and more dominant voices. Although she is very much in relationship with her family, and to a certain extent with those who care for her (despite the fact that the infection which led to her amputation was picked up in hospital), her voice was a lone voice that, if heard, was ignored. If those around her were singing in major keys, she was struggling to sing in a minor key. There was no resolution to these two contradictory voices. Her moments of stasis were experienced when she attended chapel services.

In the fourth case study (as has been already noticed), A experiences a multiplicity of voices which are best understood linearly and contrapuntally, rather than vertically and homophonically. Because of the discordant nature of these voices, musically this can perhaps best be expressed by A experiencing atonality in a perceived tonal world. She is indeed a lone voice, but a lone voice that occasionally resonates with lone voices in the Bible. But there are moments of stasis and consonance for her when she receives Holy Communion and reads narratives about the Exodus.

In the fifth case study, clearly the voices of the ward staff appear to be at complete loggerheads with the voices of their managers. In musical terms, their voices seem to be being articulated, Charles Ives-like, in completely different keys. Sadly, there was no real resolution to this polytonality. The ward staff collectively found that in relation to their managers they were a lone voice. The underlying problem seems to be that they have had no meaningful relationship with their managers in the first place.

In the sixth case study, the staff of the centre at which R1 was living were completely in harmony with the environment he required to live a fulfilling life. R1 was definitely not made to feel like a lone voice. Once he had died, this harmony became dislocated, because an important 'melodic line' had disappeared from their community. But there was a different harmony coming from Trust managers (reflecting the polytonality of the fifth case study above), where there seemed to be no meeting of minds at all. Eventually, this dominant tonality prevailed.

In the last case study, the environment of the dementia centre again meant that R2 felt cherished within it, as indeed did his wife. But her deep-seated anger can be perhaps pictured as a dissonant voice breaking away from the harmony of everything that the centre stood for. Once it had been articulated, including in the preparations for her husband's funeral, the voice of R2's widow, having been supported by the homophonic mood music of the centre, could reach a point of consonance and stasis once again.

Musical colour

In answer to the question 'Which came first the instrument or the voice?' unquestionably, the voice came first and was thus experimented with first. Instruments were initially tools, whether scraped, blown or hit, which were used as a means of aiding communication or serving a functional purpose such as assisting with hunting or stimulating pleasure. In music containing words, there has always been and will remain a debate over which of these has primacy over the other. To a large extent this will depend on the kind of music being set. If the song is sung with few accompanying instruments, in an intimate setting, especially if it is a love song, one would expect the words to take the lead. But if the idea is to draw attention to that which is beyond description, one would expect music to take the lead. And this affects the vocal colour of the piece.

In religious music of the Renaissance, sometimes the music became so florid that one could lose track of the meaning of the words to such an extent that effectively it became instrumental music for voices in which music was the centre of the worship rather than God. Composers such as Byrd and Palestrina were felt to have the balance about right by the Church authorities, especially the Council of Trent.

When music began to be used artistically, the addition of instruments happened exclusively in non-church music, church music preferring the purity of the human voice which initially in only a few cathedrals was supported by the church organ. When instruments began to be accepted in parish church music as well, the parts taken by instrument or voice were interchangeable. Because the string, woodwind and brass pitched instruments were built upon the same pattern of pitch generators as were present in human voices (from the highest to the lowest, treble, alto, tenor, bass), families of these instruments grew up in which each part could be either played or sung. In addition to the individual voices and pitched instruments, there could also be a harmony instrument capable of playing chords (e.g. guitar, lute, harpsichord, organ) holding the whole together. In the Baroque period, it was common practice in concertos for the solo part to be adapted so that it could be played by a different solo instrument, without losing any musical integrity.

From the Classical period onwards, vocal music continued to evolve a style that was distinctive from instrumental music, but individual instruments also began to evolve their own style, very much bound up with the technical evolution of the instruments themselves. (For example, the introduction of valves to brass instruments revolutionized what they were capable of playing.) And more latterly, even electronically generated sounds have been thrown into the mix. Amongst orchestral instruments especially, the different combinations employed across string, woodwind, brass and percussion sections produce differing orchestral colours. Prominence can be given to particular voices or instruments by placing them closer to, or further away from, the audience. Which instruments are being used, and whether or not they are given prominence, requires careful discernment.

REFLECTION – LISTENING TO THE COLOUR OF THE VOICE AND THE MOOD THAT LIES BEHIND IT

In the first case study, the mood of T's story is upbeat and positive but told within the overall framework of an understanding that the illness will win in the end. Whilst not overtly religious, it is highly spiritual and is articulated within the framework of decreasing time. T's story was told within his bedroom at the hospice which he made his own by putting his name on his door. It became a sanctuary for others to share their stories, the telling of his story giving permission for others to tell theirs.

In the second case study, C's parents find it hard to articulate what is on their hearts. The immediacy of funeral arrangements demanded their initial attention, but then their story is perhaps understandably told in dark hues, initial grief giving way to anger. Religious words are not used at all, but it appears that religious services of remembrance prove important to them in marking their child's existence. A story that began to be told at their child's bedside will continue to be part of who they are for the rest of their lives.

In the third case study, because S believed that she could never come to terms with her amputation, it is told in dark colours, a darkness which is compounded by a refusal by others to listen to her concerns. She tries to place what has happened to her within the context of her faith, which whilst giving her moments of solace, because she cannot really make sense of her experience within this framework, again adds to her sense of darkness. Because much of her story is told in a single room in which she is being barrier nursed, this adds to her sense of isolation.

In the fourth case study, because of the absence of many personal boundaries, paradoxically, A's story can appear to be being told in a succession of bright colours as she flits from one enthusiasm to another. Although she is unable to fully articulate what is going on in her head, she finds the language of metaphor extremely helpful. Her language is spiritual and at times religious. But it is apparent that these bright bursts of colour are framed by a feeling of isolation and darkness, rather like fireworks framed in the darkness of the night sky.

In the fifth case study, two colours predominate: the brightness of the management staff, undergirded by the certainty of their actions, and the opaque darkness of the ward staff, who initially seemed unsure how to respond. Whilst the managers clearly articulated their wishes, the ward staff struggled to articulate theirs. When they recovered their voice, they found that managers were not listening. The 'wake', which enabled ward staff both to grieve the present and to celebrate the past, is rather like voices giving way to instruments to convey that which lies beyond words.

In the sixth case study, the sadness of bereavement seems to be eclipsed by the joy of celebrating R1's life and the fact that the residential accommodation in which he had lived for many years enabled him to live such a fulfilling life. Again the language used was not religious but spiritual, marvelling at the fact that someone who appeared so disadvantaged and in need of so much help himself was able to give so much back to those who cared for him. But this celebratory brightness was itself overshadowed by the darkness of uncertainty concerning the centre's future.

The last case study reveals the opaqueness of dementia periodically giving way to moments of epiphany as memories are fleetingly remembered, such as happened for R2 at the final carol service he attended. Whilst an undergirding warmth of colour can be felt to represent an assessment centre that enables these moments to occur, any patient's death can cause this colour to darken. The death of R2 was the catalyst which precipitated the gathering of very dark storm clouds indeed for his widow. She needed to be given space to allow these to dissipate.

In exploring the act of music making with its components of pitch, tempo, dynamics, harmonic language and timbre, and applying these to the pastoral encounter, I have suggested that this can assist a person to discern their voice amidst the many other voices; become aware of its colour and the mood music that lies behind it; ascertain whether it is in harmony or in conflict with other voices; and listen to their own pulse and rhythm of life; in short (as Boyce-Tillman advocated in Chapter 3), it can help them discover their own unique voice. I shall now consider whether musical form has anything to offer by way of framing the pastoral encounter itself.

Musical form (new and repeated musical material)

In his book *The Enduring Melody*, Michael Mayne used the musical form of *cantus firmus* (enduring melody) to frame his illness of cancer whilst taking note of the enduring reality of his faith (2006, p.xviii). Whilst arguably, from a musical point of view, he could have used the forms of Ground Bass or Passacaglia to the same end, the choice has to remain his and his alone. By extending the experience of the self-framing of an illness to that of the framing of a pastoral encounter by others, my contention is that specific examples of musical form can provide helpful models for pastoral engagement (Appendix 3).

In essence, musical form lays bare music's structure, revealing how contrasting and similar material is 'collaged' in such a way that a new work of art is the result (calling to mind Bulgakov's 'antimony' to which I alluded in Chapter 3). It offers the possibility that, in pastoral care, contrasting wisdoms born of received traditions of faith and contemporary experience, rather than appearing to negate each other, through 'critical dialogue' and 'theological reflection', offer 'new insights' to both (Pattison and Lynch 2005, pp.412, 415–18). Whilst I am suggesting using examples from the world of music, others might equally well choose formal examples from architecture, the visual arts or drama. The principle remains the same: to use frames of reference from outside the world of pastoral care better to understand, inform and find ways of relating traditions of faith to contemporary experience.

Musical form falls into two groups:

Monothematic forms (where there is one main theme in evidence): Fantasia, Theme and Variations, Cantus firmus, Ground Bass, Passacaglia, Fugue

Dualistic forms (where there are two or more themes in dialogue with each other): Strophic Form, Da Capo Form, Rondo Form, Sonata Form.

The choice of which form to apply to which pastoral situation is, and has inevitably to be, a personal application. Repeated and differing themes or sections are indicated by the use of the same or different letters of the alphabet (just as in poetry, they are used to indicate rhymes). The particular forms which may prove helpful in processing the pastoral encounters contained within the seven case studies explored above can be represented by the following table:

Table 4.1 Musical forms and case studies

	Monothematic forms	Case studies
1	*Fantasia*	
2	*Theme and Variations*	*Case study 4*
3	*Fugue*	*Case study 7*
	Dualistic forms	**Case studies**
4	*AB (Strophic)*	*Case study 2*
5	*ABA (Da Capo)*	*Case study 1, Case study 6*
6	*Rondo*	*Case study 5*
7	*Sonata Form*	*Case study 3*

Case study 1 can be compared to the Da Capo (ABA) Form. In this example, the patient's positive attitude to life (and his determination to have the last laugh) is represented by A; the illness and his subsequent death by B; the patient's positive attitude to life (and his determination to have the last laugh by a third party reading out the homily that he had written for his funeral) again represented by A. The patient's positive attitude to life, even in the midst of his illness, is matched by that of his friends, many of whom, like him, were police officers, and used in their working life to supporting one another in the face of tragic circumstances, often through the use of humour. In any musical representation of this, there would have to be a jokey theme counterbalancing the tragic theme of the illness. In section B there would have to be a way of linking the patient's tragic circumstances with those of many young men killed on the Normandy beaches (possibly through calling to mind well-known war songs). There would also need to be a way of contrasting the patient's tragic terminal illness with the health of the youngsters he was coaching (possibly through juxtaposing songs from his youth with theirs). The A material might well be in a major key, and the B section in a minor key.

Case study 2 can be compared to the relatively straightforward Strophic (AB) Form in which the patient's death and bereavement of her family is represented by letter A, and the children's memorial service which grew out of it enabled others to grieve over the loss of their children who had died by letter B. This little girl's diagnosis, the amputation of her leg, the loss of her hair, her death and the grief of her family and friends are suggested in this form of differing verses having the same music but different words. The fact of three other children also being diagnosed with other cancers might suggest this music being written in four melodic lines. The anger of the parents finding a kind of transformation in the evolution of the annual children's memorial service, where those who have experienced similar bereavements come together in a gesture of mutual support, with the indication that something positive is coming out of something negative, suggests musically a minor key finding resolution in a major key.

Case study 3 fits within an extended Bridge Sonata Form (so called because if the first and second themes in the Exposition and their counterparts in the Recapitulation (in which their order of being stated is reversed) are respectively joined together by an imaginary curved line, they form an arch structure around the central Development section). In the Exposition, the importance of the patient's body image (over life) and her not wanting the operation is represented by the first theme, whilst the importance of her life (over body image) and family and doctors wanting her to have the operation by the second theme. The engagement in this argument, which reaches its climax with the amputation occurring, then constitutes the Development section. In the Recapitulation, the importance of her life (over her body image) having now become justified is the second theme, with the patient preferring to have died than having had her body mutilated, the first theme. Musically speaking, whilst the first theme in the Exposition section might well be imagined to be in a major key, because of all that happens in the Development section, and the patient's belief that she has made the wrong decision (even though it was a decision that saved her life), its appearance in the Recapitulation section might well be in a minor key, and quiet, her former courage at taking a stand being changed into resignation.

Case study 4 can be compared to a Theme and Variations. The underlying theme for the patient is her inability to process boundaries and the inevitable sense of chaos that this produces for her (unless she is in the presence of something or someone which for her emanates peace). This theme, if imagined musically, would be full of leaps and lack a meaningful tonal centre. Her abuse as a child, her hospital admission as a teenager, her spiritual confusion, her hospital admission as an adult (including her attempted suicide, which forms the basis of this case study) are all variations on this theme. The love she experienced from her grandparents, her love of stories (both as a child and as an adult), the solace she received from the sacraments and from scripture, whilst clearly being in stark contrast to these other experiences, can be understood as springing from the same lack of boundaries, as she appears to lack the psychological tools to resist either bad or good influences. Musically, these themes would be more tonally centred, more homophonic (to give a greater sense of stability), and may even include thematic references to nursery rhymes recalling the storytelling by her grandparents.

Case study 5 falls within the pattern of a Rondo. The period of stability enjoyed by the ward staff at the cottage hospital is represented by letter A, the move to the main hospital and the huge change this meant for the ward staff by letter B, the brief period of stability in their new ward home by letter A, the further chaos caused by the closure of this ward and the breakup of the staff team (even though no one was made redundant) by letter C, with the 'wake' celebrating all that the ward had represented over the years (with especial reference to the staff who had worked there, the patients who had been cared for there and their relatives who had been supported there) by letter A. Musically, theme A can be imagined as being legato (smooth notes), theme B, because of its disruption, as being staccato (short notes), with the final statement of theme A being in a minor key.

Case study 6 also fits an extended Da Capo (A1BA2) Form where the patient, when alive, is represented by A1, his death and the making of funeral arrangements by B, with the staff's recollections of their deceased client, of whom they were clearly very fond, by A2. Because of the client's severe learning disability, any musical representation of his interaction with those around him might be depicted employing extremes of contrast and dissonance. As with the previous case study, humour would need to feature in this section, as would melodic references to transport in general and the RAF in particular. Section B would be likely to be meditative, employ no extremes of contrast and would be far more consonant, the death of a much loved client heralding changes in the provision of care for those with learning disability and thus mark a double ending. With the reprise of the A material, there is a sense that ending though this may be, no one can take away the unique memories shared between this client and his carers, who by default had become his extended family. In musical terms, it feels as though A1 would be in a minor key and A2 in its relative major key.

Case study 7 can be compared to a Fugue, in which the patient's diminishing periods of clarity, such as engaging with past memories, with the outside world and with the eternal memory of God, provide the fugal material, with his ever-present, and ever-increasing dementia providing the episodic material. Although his dementia comes to an end with his death, within the context of faith there is the hope that earthly death brings with it a healing of memories (symbolized musically by a complete reiteration of the fugal statement). But because, for his wife, his dementia was seen as yet one more way in which her husband could be persecuted (a persecution which she vicariously shared), her anger at his life and his death perpetuated a sense of fragmentation beyond his death. This might be a fugue which ends with episodic material rather than a reiteration of the fugue.

*

In this section, I have sought to suggest that, in an attempt to frame pastoral encounters, music seems to lend itself not only to the holding together of opposites but to the enabling of dialogue to take place, irrespective of whether there is any resolution of these opposing perspectives. Whilst considering whether specific examples of musical form can provide helpful models for pastoral engagement, it is very important to remember that these engagements remain pastoral encounters and never become staged performances. In the immediacy of the pastoral encounter, one is always listening out for the voice of God.

Conclusion: The writing down of music – the musical score as a spiritual care plan

By continuing to employ music as a dialogue partner, this chapter has suggested that just as the application of contrasting musical polarities and musical form has assisted in bringing a renewed sense of discernment to the seven case studies considered earlier, so having this better discernment of sameness and difference may have something helpful to say about what is being voiced (or remaining unvoiced) within the pastoral encounter. To assist in this process, I would further suggest that just as music (as with all language), whilst it began as an oral and aural tradition, as it passed down through the generations became more complex, and so a way had to be found of recording it by writing it down, so too is the case with recording pastoral encounters. As I have suggested viewing pastoral 'music making' through the musical prisms of pitch, tempo, dynamics, harmonic language, timbre and musical form, some kind of musical notation itself may prove helpful in this regard. Or another could be used or invented that covered the same categories. Thus framed, the pastoral care encounter, which so often can appear chaotic and reactive, is ordered and has the potential to be better informed and enlightened, and thus better understood.

5

LISTENING TO THE VOICE OF PASTORAL EXPERIENCE

(2) Classical Music as a Vehicle for
Theoretical and Practical Transformation

The pastoral carer as a participant and interpreter in pastoral 'music making'

In continuing the process of employing music as a dialogue partner, this chapter explores whether the use of musical participation can provide a possible model for pastoral caring, and musical interpretation a model for pastoral discernment. In imagining practical theology as an orchestra in which received tradition and contemporary experience are performed, the pastoral carer is imagined variously as conductor, performance space, listener, as well as co-performer. Although the focus of the pastoral care relationship considered below continues to be that exercised within healthcare, those insights gleaned from musical performance are equally applicable to other pastoral care situations.

Musical participation as a possible model for pastoral caring

Stevenson-Moessner's use of the metaphor of music on the wider theological stage, in her transposition of Anton Boisen's 'living human documents' into 'living human instruments', applies the metaphor of orchestra to practical theology. For her, practical theology is an orchestra which is concerned with harmonious relationships with other 'musicians' (those practitioners of various theological disciplines and those caught up in the organization of parish life), not appearing 'as soloist or guest musician' but playing 'in concert' with them, with, most importantly for this present discussion, the minister as the conductor (2008, p.1). Sometimes this engagement can be discordant and cacophonous, but 'cacophony precedes harmony and creation' (p.x). For her, in this metaphor, 'theology is the music of religious enquiry' (p.1). Thus practical theology is conceived as a spiritual symphony that collages faith and action, putting faith into action and action into faith. It offers connectedness not only to other disciplines but within its own (p.69). Just as the minister is seen as the link between the 'various theological disciplines' and present pastoral engagement, so, within the hospital context, the healthcare chaplain can be a link between non-theological professional healthcare staff and the pastoral encounter.

Frances Young drew a parallel between performance and hermeneutics (by way of broadening the question concerning the authority of scripture thrown up by the application of literary criticism to its texts), by asking: 'How can we perform the Bible – in a modern world so different from the past which produced and used it?' (1990, p.1). Whence lies its inspiration? Influenced by Koestler, Young believes that there is a kind of inspiration which is born 'of previously unrelated frames of reference or universes of discourse – whose union will solve the previously insoluble problem' (Koestler 1964, cited in Young 1990, p.2). Once again (recalling Bulgakov's views in Chapter 3 above), meaning, as does inspiration, lies beyond perceived contradictions between texts, and beyond those between traditions of faith and current experiences.

David Lyall, in effect, asks a similar question of pastoral care as Young asks of hermeneutics above. How can we perform pastoral care in a modern world so different from the past? He understands pastoral care to be 'a creative art', which similarly is able 'to tolerate ambiguity and ambivalence…that awakens the imagination and evokes awareness of new possibilities' (2000, p.311). One response to this is modelling pastoral care following the pattern of musical improvisation. But, as Lyall continues, 'Sometimes situations are of such ethical complexity that there is no obvious right thing to do; sometimes life is so tragic that there is nothing to be said which will "make things better"' (p.311). But even in simply being there, 'the toleration of ignorance (of itself) becomes an enabling grace' (p.317). Then, as in hermeneutics, so too in pastoral care, 'only in the empty space created by God can a resolution of human strife be played out.

Only in the empty space that *is* God can the drama be truly holy and the invisible be made visible' (Young 1990, p.191; emphasis added).

The chaplain (pastoral carer) as conductor

Stevenson-Moessner's idea of 'living human instruments' hints that music might have something to offer the players in the pastoral care encounter, as what can be true of the macrocosm, can also be true for the microcosm (2008 p.xiii). In seeing 'the theological, christological import of the position of conductor', she believes that 'God or Christ may be seen as a unique realization of this creative co-ordinator, the conductor'. But she understands the conductor as performing a 'non-hierarchical role', thereby seeing it as a helpful 'model for practical theological leadership (p.54). If Christ is understood as a conductor, so much more so must be his ministers. If the minister (chaplain) is seen as conductor, and the role of the conductor is, as Hunter asserts, to 'orchestrate', read and understand the music, know its history and its meanings, give attention to nuances and subtleties and enable the playing by the orchestra of a great symphony (Hunter 2004, p.128, cited in Stevenson-Moessner 2008, p.54), then the chaplain has to illustrate the qualities of 'involved detachment and critical responsibility' (Woodward 2000, p.17). The conductor is forever listening critically to that which is being performed.

In a healthcare environment that is becoming increasingly secular and where faith-neutral spirituality is gaining more credibility than religious faith, it is vital that healthcare chaplains remain theologically grounded. If not, they run the real risk of having nothing theologically helpful to say at all and of their presence within healthcare becoming superfluous. The challenge for healthcare chaplains, operating a theological model of chaplaincy within an environment with secular expectations, is how to speak from that faith tradition in situations of brokenness and pain. Clearly, what chaplains believe underpins how they act; what they encounter in their pastoral relationships informs what they believe. I am suggesting that the chaplain is called upon to model nothing less than God him/herself, a God who can be seen, through the chaplain's presence at the bedside and elsewhere, to be involved with, and supportive of, humanity in the midst of its suffering. By practising the art of being 'present', the chaplain's presence can become sacramental, experienced as an 'outward and visible sign of an inward and spiritual grace' (thus echoing the definition of the sacraments in the Catechism; BCP 1970, p.356).

In a healthcare environment in which the concept of health is viewed with increasing degrees of fragmentation, it is also vital that healthcare chaplains remain inclusively holistically grounded, in touch with the musical idea of communal performance. If health is not seen in terms of a communal performance with a number of different performers (including the patients themselves) with different parts to play within the healthcare score, the patient has no chance of maintaining their sense of personhood. This multi-layered communal performance enables the keeping alive of hope with the possibility of transformation, the adherence to a faith. It gives permission for people to be and become themselves, all of which takes place within the music of affirming (sometimes even loving) relationships mirroring the unconditional love God has for his people. It points to the enfleshing of God in situations of brokenness and weakness.

Each successive pastoral encounter requires the chaplain to reflect theologically upon it. To encourage this process of theological reflection, chaplains need to be in touch with those skilled in listening to their own 'cries from the heart' arising from the collage of experience with received tradition. This will help them to search authentically and possibly discern the presence of God. It will help them guard against the very real danger of being seduced by the 'cries from the head' arising out of the secular institution in which they are working, in which God, whose existence is never acknowledged, can only be perceived as being absent. The chaplain is tasked with being a facilitator of meaning, assisting in the letting go of old symbols and helping in the discovery of new ones through which new meanings and new ways of thinking about God are brought to birth.

The chaplain (pastoral carer) as the performance space

But there are other musical functions that can also bring clarity to the nature of the pastoral relationship in which chaplains are involved. Chaplains can be compared to the space in which music is performed. In attentively listening to another person, chaplains can find themselves being used as performance spaces in which what should be shared and what should remain private are being worked out, and tested. Chaplains can also be expected to facilitate that which is being shared and must themselves decide how best to manage the material shared within the pastoral encounter. Chaplains must also decide how much they share of themselves in the process. In short, chaplains can find themselves tasked with the management of boundaried space, within which meaning-making can begin to take place. It is the presence of chaplains themselves that offers patients and staff a spiritual performing space in which unrecognized feelings can be recovered and then rehearsed, where people can tell or re-frame their stories and in the telling of those stories find healing.

In order for a chaplaincy to work effectively in hospital, it is vital that the chaplain has open access to the patients in their care (unless there is a medical reason which prohibits this, or the patient has specifically requested that they do not receive chaplaincy visits). Adequate time needs to be made available to enable chaplaincy visits to take place. Ward staff need to understand the role that chaplaincy plays in the overall health and wellbeing of the patient, so that pastoral conversations are not interrupted unnecessarily. An adequate area needs to be set aside for functioning as a quiet room, so that if the patient is well enough to leave their bed, confidential conversations can be conducted there. Away from the ward, there need to be ample opportunities for patients, their relatives or members of staff to have access to a chaplain. There need to be designated quiet areas, such as a chaplaincy office, chapel, multi-faith room, counselling or interview rooms, in which confidential conversations can be conducted by chaplains and others.

A designated chapel space also provides a location in which liturgy, especially that which arises out of a specific pastoral need, can take place. This enables individuals, and the communities of which they are a part, to engage, unlock, become involved with, and to own the meaning of the situations and texts with which they come into contact. This is possible because liturgy provides a medium for holding in a safe place that which is almost too hard to bear and offers the hope of transforming it. Chaplains should seek to explain the need for, and value of, protected private space for some aspects of pastoral care delivery. Having done this, chaplains then need to reclaim this spiritual space both philosophically, and practically, within the healthcare Trusts in which they work.

The work of chaplaincy itself takes place in the large performing space of public liturgy and various healthcare committee meetings and the smaller space of bedside ministry. As the spiritual performing space, the chaplain provides for the patient a safe place in which unrecognized feelings can be recovered and then rehearsed, where 'immersion in the wounded scar of damaged tissue can take place, out of which healing comes and to which it goes' (Boyce-Tillman 2000, p.282). The chaplain offers a place where people can tell their stories, and, by doing so, gives permission for people to do so, so that they may let go of their demons, in the telling of those stories find healing, and learn to play (perform) once again. In doing this, chaplains are simply following the pattern of Jesus' disciples who, by telling their story, invite us to enable others to tell their story.

The chaplain (pastoral carer) as an attentive listener

Chaplains must be proactive in rediscovering what it means to really listen to another person. To make this point might at first seem something of an oxymoron as listening is so key to the pastoral task. Attentive listening is particularly crucial in Carl Rogers' psychological approach of the 1940s and in Lake's Clinical Theology of the 1960s and 1970s. This kind of listening is particularly important for those trying to process life-changing experiences, especially when that involves grieving over a loved one's death, attentive listening being nothing less than loving courtesy. Insights from music make clear that, as well as being attentive, listening must be reflective and thus occasionally critical. As was noted in Chapter 4, musical listening is concerned with listening to more than one strand at a time: listening to melody, harmony, rhythm, timbre, locating the current voice within a community or even a cacophony of voices, staying with the chaos, locating the 'now' with 'what has been' and 'with what may be', so that one's contribution, when made, because it is attentive, sacrificial and focused, is appropriate and timely. Also important is listening to what is not being said (the musical rests) as was noted above in Chapter 4. Listening to what the whole person is saying leads to what Swinton describes as nothing less than the 'resurrection of the person' (2000, p.10).

Furthermore, just as the context in which musicians perform and an audience listens can affect the way music is interpreted, so too can the spatial and temporal context of a pastoral conversation affect its interpretation. Critical listening is not just the prerogative of the pastoral carer, the auditor. As with music, so too it must be undertaken by the talker, the performer within the pastoral care setting. As well as being attentive and critical, listening must also remain detached. Paradoxically, just as too much listening can get in the way of music-making, so too over-involved listening can blunt effective pastoral care. As with music, it can prevent the pastoral carer, and therefore the pastoral relationship itself, from moving forward, being understood as gift and being lived in the present. In order to remain an abiding presence within healthcare, chaplains must be theologically rooted, bearing within themselves the memory of crucifixion and resurrection. Chaplains must themselves be connected to something of the numinous if they are to have any chance of enabling others to do likewise. To use a phrase from Kenneth Stevenson, effective pastoral care requires the pastoral carer to be 'rooted in detachment' so that listening becomes a process of discernment in which cloud gives way to transfiguration, the cloud both obscuring and representing 'the presence of God' (2007, p.98). It is only when people are listened to attentively that meaning-making has any chance of beginning. The chaplain, from the perspective of Holy Saturday, offers the pastoral upbeat of resurrection hope.

The chaplain (pastoral carer) as a co-performer

Chaplains must pay attention to the person who is performing, by providing a relational bridge through which a person may articulate their innermost redemptive desires. In the act of listening to another's stories, the chaplain must strive to discern God's presence within them. To be effective pastoral carers, as well as being effective auditors, chaplains must also be drawn into performance themselves, responding to the cries arising out of the pastoral encounter and those arising from the tradition of faith, the one empowering the other, and God being in them both, ensuring that a continual dialogue inevitably takes place between them. The patient's performance, their 'cry of the heart', is nothing less than a demand for wisdom, a demand for understanding amidst the chaos of living (Ford 2007, p.5). Because of the chaplain who truly listens, the patient is able to articulate that his or her performance is 'not a *flight from* the world of pain and matter but a *mission into* it' (Vanier 2004, p.13; emphasis added). Through the chaplain's attentiveness, affirmation is given to patients who are encouraged to believe, and apply to themselves, that the central tenet of the human condition is to accept and love oneself. Both music and pastoral care exist within the present moment, the relationship between teller (performer) and hearer (listener) continually coming alive in each successive present moment.

Musical interpretation as model for pastoral discernment

In seeking to discern the presence of God not only in a 'received tradition' but also in a lived contemporary experience, this study has so far traced a path which indicates that, both theologically and musically, belief in God can only have any credibility if God can be seen to be involved with, and supportive of, humanity in the midst of its suffering. Clearly, this is not a new theological insight, but what it does underline is that those who experience periods of profound darkness in their lives have to embark on a journey from loss of meaning to meaning-making, a journey which discovers wisdom emerging out of lament. Having been thrown into a time of existential crisis, as they begin to try to make sense of what is going on in their lives, they are brought into contact with those world views which, for the person of faith, will include sacred texts and the wider faith tradition. This may prove immediately helpful, and meaning may dawn once again. But if this fails to engage with where people find themselves, this juxtaposition of opposing world views can exacerbate loss of meaning. What it can also do, however, is to begin a reaction arising out of these opposing views that needs to be articulated and heard by someone else as the existence of a reality that lies beyond that which is immediately apparent. In the musical compositions considered above, disparate texts and disparate musical ideas (and a combination of both of these) were collaged together in such a way that the artist holding up a mirror to the world resulted either in acknowledging the suffering that they are witnessing, and reflecting what is seen or heard, or searching in them for a way of surviving the horrors that they are observing and offering hope to a troubled world. But the very act of holding disparate ideas together in collage of itself offers the seeds of transformation. Within the hospital setting it is often the chaplain who strives to hear what the patient has to say to them, and this within the chaplain's own framework of faith. This requires attentive listening not just to what is being said but also to what is not being said (in musical terms, the rests), and what is being said metaphorically.

As the (patient's) need for conceptual and existential reorientation takes hold, this may require a response which needs some kind of attentive working out liturgically (as was noticed in case studies 2, 6 and 7 above). This may not invariably require a public act of worship in the chapel, but could be carried out privately with patients at their bedside (as in case studies 1, 3 and 4). It may not need any overtly religious liturgy at all but some more secular 'acting out' (as in case study 5). This will either lead to some kind of meaning being discovered or a loss of meaning still pertaining, in which case opportunities need to be created for this cycle to begin again. But it is not exclusively the chaplain who is the primary hearer of the patient's yearning for meaning-making; part of the role of the chaplain is also to facilitate this process in others.

Drawing upon the Hermeneutical Cycle applied to the text (Carr 1997, pp.22–7), and the Pastoral Cycle, applied to situations (Green 1990, pp.25–30), in which each successive new approach to a text or pastoral situation is shaped by previous experiences of looking at it, and reflecting upon it; this meaning-making journey can be expressed in the form of a Meaning-Making Cycle and be summarized as follows:

Meaning/loss of meaning → Juxtaposition/correlation → Attentive (metaphorical) listening → Attentive (liturgical) working out/ performative theology → Loss of meaning/meaning.

These three approaches can be juxtaposed and compared in the following table:

Table 5.1 Cycle comparisons

Hermeneutical Cycle (Carr 1997, pp.22–7)	Pastoral Cycle (Green 1990, pp.25–30)	Meaning-Making Cycle (Clifton-Smith 2013)
'approach the text'	'experience'	Meaning/loss of meaning
'get inside the text'	'exploration'	Juxtaposition/ correlation
'become involved in the meaning'	'reflection'	Attentive (metaphorical) listening
'be transformed'	'response'	Attentive (liturgical) working out/ performative theology
'prepare to approach the text anew'	'new situation' which must be experienced afresh	Loss of meaning/ meaning

These three models advocate practical ways of 'doing' theology by each looking at the interplay between Scripture, Tradition and Reason ('the three pillars on which Anglican thinking rests' (Carr 1997, p.22)).

For Carr, the hermeneutical process begins when a biblical text needs not just to be read but actively interpreted by the reader, the process of interpretation being concerned with 'the dynamic interchange between text and reader' (p.22). This interchange can proceed in one of two ways: by 'putting questions to the text, as a result of which the questions are reshaped and asked anew', or 'by understanding its component parts which can…only be understood by reference to the whole' (p.23). Either way, to 'get inside the text, to become involved in the meaning' through this interactive process leads to the reader being 'transformed'. Scripture may contain 'eternal truths', but its texts are 'time-limited' and require unlocking, whether that be in an individual or group setting (pp.24, 26).

For Green, 'this whole reflective exercise is best not done in isolation' but in the company of others as 'theology is an activity of the whole body of Christ' (1990, p.28). The process of theological reflection begins when 'there is a situation that confronts us or an activity to cope with', either of which 'will have the common element of worry or anguish about it' (p.25). Because 'no one comes to the experience from a vacuum', we need 'to explore some of our prior feelings and prejudices, for good or ill, about the experience or issue' (p.26). We then need to undertake 'a thorough analysis of the situation in which it is set', using 'all the disciplines at our disposal' (p.26). Then 'the situation being experienced must be brought into direct intimate contact with the Christian faith and all that the Christian community means for us' (p.29). Then, 'in the light of all the experience, exploration and reflection', the group has to respond: 'What does God now require of us?' (p.29).

The Meaning-Making Cycle combines the reflective approach of the Hermeneutical Cycle with the pastoral encounter present within the Pastoral Cycle. Preferring to regard hermeneutics as 'an art' rather than 'a science' (Carr 1997, p.23), it uses the discipline of music as an analytical tool as one of 'the disciplines at our disposal' (Green 1990, p.26) to avoid the danger of individualizing the pastoral encounter and separating it from the wider community of faith and experience (after Green 1990, p.28). It roots the whole encounter within the 'the dynamic interchange' of performance (Carr 1997, p.22). As with the Hermeneutical and Pastoral Cycles, the Meaning-Making Cycle can be understood in terms of a spiral, with each new 'performance' building on and learning from the previous one and ready to engage with the next 'Loss of Meaning' episode. Thus the Meaning-Making Cycle can also be expressed in the following diagram:

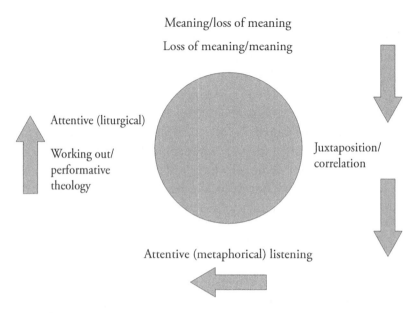

Figure 5.1 Meaning-Making Cycle

As with music, so too in the pastoral situation, the application of attentive listening has initiated a performative response. What are then underlying aspects of the Meaning-Making Cycle as depicted in the diagram above?

1. Meaning and loss of meaning

The question of whether one is able to attribute meaning to one's life or not seems to occur either when one is experiencing a period of change in one's life or when one is not. Shapiro and Carr believe that '[i]nterpreting the situation afresh' is key to rediscovering meaning (1991, p.145). This is nowhere more apparent than when a person has been bereaved and the relations and functions within the family unit have to be reinterpreted in the light of the person who has died. Perhaps there is no more disorganized or fragmented state than that of dementia, and therefore no greater yearning for meaning-making than those suffering from, or those watching their loved one suffering from, this illness (as was noted in case study 7 above). Yet (as was mentioned in Chapter 2) it is possible to view dementia in a different light.

Interpreting situations afresh in order to discern meaning in them is often inhibited if one appeals to the intellect alone, just as it would be if one appeals to the senses alone. Indeed, there are times when the use of words alone can be confusing, when one recognizes the depth of an emotion but finds oneself unable to express it. If one has no way of describing any given experience, one has no chance of attributing meaning to it. The use of metaphors or symbols can be extremely helpful here, a subject made all the more urgent by many previously familiar symbols and metaphors having become meaningless, and there is the need to reinvent symbols when they are no longer working, a subject to which I will return later in this chapter.

The meaning of an individual's experience is directly affected by the community or communities of which the individual feels themselves to be a part, as is the collective experience of the community by the experience of its constituent members. Meaning is transformed when health is understood holistically. Within the Christian community of faith, it is vital to keep the 'crucifixion' of experience framed within 'resurrection' hope. Keeping the crucifixion and the resurrection in dialogue with each other, exploring whether a variety of voices are rooted in Babel or Pentecost, is what the musical compositions examined in Chapter 3 above sought to do. They variously juxtapose: temporality and eternity, poetry and requiem mass, accounts of desolation and biblical and prayer book texts, sameness and difference. One (Tippett's *A Child of Our Time*) juxtaposes narrative and spiritual. Indeed, the spirituals themselves juxtapose the journey from slavery to freedom of the Jewish people with that of African people. All of these compositions seek to explore the 'wound', the 'crack in the fabric' that is situated between Good Friday and Easter Day, and, in so doing, give meaning to both.

2. Juxtaposition and correlation

Central to the discipline of practical theology, and to this present study, is how disparate sources of material relate to each other, most especially traditional and contemporary material. The beginnings of correlation can be found in the theology of Thomas Aquinas (1225–1274), which was itself 'founded on the synthesis of Christian theology with Aristotelean philosophy' (Graham, Walton and Ward 2005, p.144). In the nineteenth century it was associated with Friedrich Daniel Ernst Schleiermacher (1768–1834), in the mid-twentieth century the correlative method was developed by Paul Tillich (1886–1965), Seward Hiltner (1909–1984) and David Tracy (b.1939) through whom a change can be traced in the relationship between traditional and contemporary material where the latter comes into the ascendancy. There was also a change in the direction in which wisdom was perceived to flow: from one way to flowing in both directions. Following their example, the way forward is not to allow one or other of these aspects to dominate in the theological relationship, but, through the medium of 'collage', to nurture the energy that can be generated between them. In providing a medium for 'critical dialogue' and 'theological reflection' to germinate, as it has already been noted, the opportunity is generated for 'new insights' to emerge (Pattison and Lynch 2005, pp.412, 415–18).

Music provides such a medium (noticed above in Chapter 3), as it 'requires the ability to express oneself with absolute commitment and passion whilst listening carefully and sensitively to another voice which may even contradict one's own statement' (Barenboim 2008, cited in Winkett 2010, p.77). As in music, 'the process of integration…[can be] seen as the state of the peaceful co-existence of diversity' (Boyce-Tillman 2000, p.245), so pastoral care needs, in the words of Frances Young, 'to hold two sides of an issue in tension over and over again… to have room for a sense of complexity and mystery, even of apparent paradox' (1991, p.235).

3. Attentive metaphorical listening

We saw above how attentive listening requires not just 'listening to what *is* being said but also to what *is not* being said'. Because 'sometimes the difficulty of recounting painful experiences is born of an inability to attribute meaning to them', symbols and metaphors can be a way of engaging with an experience. Sometimes metaphorical language can help (see McFague 1983, p.15). At other times, the use of symbols can be of assistance (see Williams 1983, p.283). Of particular interest in this study (especially in relation to case study 4) is the ability of symbols and metaphors to help individuals unlock, become involved with, and own the meaning of the situations and texts with which they engage. Sometimes they provide a source of stability within a world that appears to be in a great state of flux.

As well as a way of communicating better and understanding one another within the pastoral setting, this approach can also benefit our understanding of written material, particularly parables. In advocating the use of the intuitive over and above the rational function of the brain when looking at a biblical text, David Lyall believes that Walter Brueggemann's approach and his 'use and development of the imagination (which) becomes a primary way of knowing' can be extremely productive (2001, p.82). Lyall argues that the metaphorical nature of parables has much to tell us in this respect, as they can be regarded as 'stories about ordinary things with the power to disclose the nature of reality' (1995, p.13). Furthermore, 'it is not simply that the pastoral *conversation* must be interpreted metaphorically and parabolically, but also the pastoral *relationship* has a parabolic character through which the Grace of God shines through' (p.13; emphasis added).

As has been seen above, music can operate metaphorically by unlocking, and thereby discerning, the meaning of a situation, be a bridge to past memories and act as an anointer or a healer of wounds. But music can also draw attention to pain and suffering (caused by the dichotomy between what should be and what is) when enfleshing the reality that 'the sound is an audible scar of damaged tissue underneath' (Winkett 2010, p.5). As was noted above (in Chapter 3), in music one way that this scar or wound can be represented is through dissonance. But just as a wound can be represented through dissonance, so musical healing can be represented through consonance. This was the position adopted by Boyce-Tillman in *Space for Peace* in which (with the Shalom chant and her own chants, all of which are in D minor and seem to harmonize one with the other), she establishes a sense of consonance. As with music, so too in pastoral care. Each generation needs to discover afresh its own metaphors and symbols. The chaplain is tasked with being a facilitator of meaning and an agent of recontextualization, assisting in the letting go of old metaphors and symbols and helping in the discovery of new ones through which new meanings and new ways of thinking about God are brought to birth.

4. Liturgy (attentive liturgical working out) and performative theology

Liturgy provides one particular way of exercising symbolic and metaphorical functions. It does this by enabling individuals, and the communities of which they are a part, to engage, unlock, become involved with, and to own the meaning of the situations and texts with which they come into contact – in other words, enflesh 'performative knowledge' in performative pastoral care (Graham, Walton, and Ward 2005, p.170). This is possible because liturgy provides a medium for holding in a safe place that which is almost too hard to bear and offers out the hope of transforming it. Shapiro and Carr refer to this as a 'holding environment', which provides 'empathic interpretation and tolerance and containment' in which difficult feelings 'can be addressed through ritualistic symbolic structure that enables chaotic experiences to be faced' (1991, p.160). An act of worship can thus be a symbolic 'holding environment' within which the 'transitions of life' can be affirmed and worked through, articulating feelings of sadness as well as celebration (p.36). Part of the process of engaging in performative pastoral care rooted in a faith tradition is to reflect theologically upon a given historical or contemporaneous situation or text, and in so doing offer an interpretation which can either be accepted or rejected.

As well as providing an '"umbilical cord" to the sacred' (Begbie 2000, p.136), liturgy also can act as a bridge to past memories. Sometimes it will serve as a healer of wounds. Sometimes, however, as was noted in the *War Requiem*, no unlocking occurs through the words of the requiem mass as there is the perception that ritual itself (or more specifically church ritual) is also dead. This in turn leads back to a sense that the ritual itself, and the liturgy contained within it, has to change. Just as music itself can be understood as a kind of performative theology, I would go further, and maintain that liturgy and pastoral care are inextricably connected, the former being the outworking and response to the latter (just as I shall argue in the next chapter that mission and pastoral care are similarly inextricably connected). This applies irrespective of whether the liturgy is religious or secular (as a rite of passage in nature) or is worked out in the public or private space (including the pastoral care relationship itself).

Clearly, there is a very close connection between liturgy and music. The fact of being involved in liturgy can of itself be therapeutic and transformative. It can be redemptive. In the *War Requiem*, for example, it was noted above how the 'Sanctus' and 'Benedictus' are messages of serene joy, even in a mass for the dead (Evans 1979, p.460). Sometimes a liturgy at which one is present, like listening to music, can conjure up a particular mood, which can find release in the remembrance of previous liturgies. Liturgy, like music, can bring a sense of structure to chaotic personal experiences and can provide the framework in which a person can tell their story (Frank 1997, p.24). It can lift the spirit, but sometimes it can have quite the reverse effect as internal pain is released and tears can flow, in which case liturgy can prove liberative. Young has said that 'Story making is a step on the road to abstract analysis and story telling the most effective way of communicating collective experience and values' (1991, p.2). Perhaps liturgy, like music, is essential, because it facilitates both 'story making' and 'story telling', the very building blocks of performative theology. That is nothing less than the ability to be open to the possibility of reappraising one's priorities, to be open to the possibility of meaning-making.

Conclusion

This chapter has continued to look at whether pastoral care has any lessons to learn from the world of music. It has explored musical participation as a possible model for pastoral caring, by examining the model of chaplain as conductor, concert hall/chamber music salon performance space, and audience; and of the chaplain and the patient as co-performers caught up in the co-equal performance of a duet. It has explored musical interpretation as a model for pastoral discernment, by merging the hermeneutic and pastoral cycles into the performative meaning-making cycle.

The Meaning-Making Cycle differs from the Hermeneutical and Pastoral Cycles in that, drawing upon the world of music making, it incorporates listening and performing. These two activities of listening and performing, reflecting and acting, are intricately bound together, but because they lead to change (like the Hermeneutical and Pastoral Cycles), as was noticed earlier in this chapter, the Meaning-Making

Cycle is not strictly circular but more like a spiral (Green 1990, p.25). Just as perfect meaning-making, like the perfect performance, is never achievable, the pastoral encounter can be understood as being comparable with the act of music making itself.

6

RECLAIMING AND PROCLAIMING PASTORAL CARE

Singing the Praises of Pastoral Care in a Mission-Focused Environment

Just as music (as a dialogue partner) has been used as a paradigm for how the past (a received tradition) can relate to the present (a lived contemporary experience), so in this chapter it is used as a model of how the future (the mission-focused ministry of the Church) can relate to the present (a lived contemporary experiential ministry of pastoral care). Because there is a perception that the performance of pastoral care is in danger of being drowned out by the Church's present preoccupation with mission, by comparing this present phenomenon with David Lyall's defence of pastoral care in the light of 'the coming of the (pastoral) counsellors', this chapter attempts similarly to defend pastoral care from the march of 'the 'mission-minded managers', a phrase coined by Martyn Percy. In so doing, it begins to explore whether pastoral care can bring a sense of 'theoretical and practical transformation' to mission itself.

By using as a framework *The Parable of the Song Smith* (which is based on the Parable of the Sower; see Appendix 4), the 'coming of the counsellors' is compared to a harmony without melody (a depth without breadth); the march of 'the mission-minded managers' is compared to a melody without harmony (a breadth without depth). It is only the provision of attentive pastoral care comparable with harmony and melody in equal measure (depth and breadth), 'incarnating the goodness of God's love for the sake of the world' (Heywood 2011, p.113), that has the potential to offer an integrated holistic pastoral performance.

The 'coming of the counsellors' (Lyall 1995, p.23ff)

At a time when pastoral counselling was in danger of overshadowing pastoral care, David Lyall proved to be a tremendous advocate for pastoral care which, he maintained, although being inherently distinct from pastoral counselling, could contain elements of counselling within it. Lyall regarded pastoral care as being 'a discipline in its own right' and not merely the poor relation of the latter, and as containing within it a 'relationship between belief and practice', which is very much a 'two-way street', both having the capacity to challenge each other, which of course is the very bedrock of practical theology (Lyall 2001, pp.20–1). But he also viewed pastoral care as having 'an integrative function in relation to much of the life of the Church' (pp.20–1).

For Lyall, pastoral care must:

1. be located within a community of faith (otherwise it cannot be pastoral)

2. be sensitive to the uniqueness of each person's spiritual journey and of 'their freedom to make their own choices'

3. take 'seriously the social and political context of care', as pastoral care is not about 'merely adjustment to, but transformation of society'.

Pastoral care can, but is not bound to:

1. 'draw upon the traditional resources of the community of faith'

2. 'take the form of a more intense pastoral counselling relationship'.

(2001, p.12)

Campbell, Pattison believed, echoed these sentiments, maintaining that in pastoral counselling, whilst there was an emphasis on 'pathology, individualism and narcism, in pastoral care Campbell wanted to transform Christian ministry into something broader, more holistic, more political and more theological' (Pattison 2008, p.7).

Although working in a one-to-one situation, Campbell (and, as will be seen below, Pattison himself) wanted pastoral care to 'also lead to challenging and transforming social structures when they colluded with sin and oppression', echoing Lyall's point above (Pattison 2008, p.7).

Pastoral care has been variously described as consisting of:

1. 'helping acts done by representative Christian persons, directed towards the healing, sustaining, guiding and reconciling of troubled persons whose trouble arises in the context of ultimate meaning and concerns' (Clebsch and Jaekle 1975, cited in Pattison 1988, p.12)

2. 'helping acts done by representative Christian persons, directed towards the healing, sustaining, guiding, *nurturing* and reconciling of troubled persons whose trouble arises in the context of ultimate meaning and concerns' (amended by Clinebell 1984, p.43)

3. 'that activity undertaken especially by representative Christian persons directed towards the elimination of sin and sorrow and the presentation of all people perfect in Christ to God' (Pattison 1988, p.13)

4. 'the establishment of a relationship or relationships whose purpose may encompass support in a time of trouble and personal and spiritual growth through deeper understanding of oneself, other and/or God. Pastoral care will have at its heart the affirmation of meaning and worth of persons and will endeavour to strengthen their ability to respond creatively to whatever life brings' (Lyall 2001, p.12).

These definitions range from the specifically Christian through to the generically human, from the communal to the individualistic. Each stresses different aspects of pastoral care and not all are in agreement with each other. Interestingly, Pattison's definition came out of his criticizing the Clebsch and Jaekle definition, because he felt that it was:

a. too clerical, and problem centred rather than growth centred, pastoral care having a relevance for all people whether troubled or not;

b. that it was individualistic rather than communal, shy of using the wider Church as a resource,

c. in danger of ruling out pastoral need that didn't have its origins in the context of ultimate meanings and concerns.

(Pattison 1988, p.13)

At a time when pastoral care is in danger of being overshadowed by strategies of mission, does another reassessment of pastoral care need to take place?

Have we reached a point in time where Campbell's definition of pastoral care of having one 'fundamental aim to know love, both as something to be received and something to give' is no longer 'surprisingly simple' but over-simplistic and is in need of further explanation (Campbell 1985, cited in Pattison 1988, p.16)?

Have we reached a point where a way needs to be found for the wider Church to acknowledge that pastoral relationships can give 'an embodied witness to the loving presence of God in the midst of ordinary human life' in times of sorrow and in times of joy (Whipp 2013, p.106)?

Have we reached a point for those involved in pastoral care to acknowledge that the context for this embodiment, out of which it springs and which it resources, is 'the Body of Christ', the Church (Percy 2013)?

My contention is that the point has indeed been reached, which will be clear in the light of the Church's call to mission, considered in the following section, where pastoral care does need to be reimagined, for both the wider Church and for those involved in pastoral care. For both, this has the potential to be transformational.

The march of the 'mission-minded managers' (Percy 2014b)

What do we mean by mission?

Mission has been traditionally understood as having to do with conveying a message or carrying out a task. Within a religious context, it has to do with a faith community propagating its own particular faith in other communities. In terms of the Christian faith, it has been traditionally understood as propagating the Christian faith among non-Christian people. It thus has primarily been understood as being action-based. Like the word 'missile' (to which it sounds so alarmingly similar), this kind of mission can be defined as delivering a targeted package with maximum force. The force with which it is delivered can be made all the more insidiously effective by the certainty that it is right!

The undertaking of mission today is invariably affected by how mission has been undertaken in the past. Although from a Christian perspective we might also understand mission as 'sharing the good news of Jesus', because it is fallible human beings who are doing the sharing, inevitably, sometimes 'bad news' can get mixed up with it. So on the back of good news can come bad news, such as abuse of power, racism, anti-Semitism, misogyny, the oppression of children and homophobia. One of the disadvantages of Constantine adopting Christianity as the official religion of the Roman Empire was that it provided a way for political power inextricably to be linked with religious certainty. So, at its worst, this volatile mix has led to the Crusades, the Inquisition, ethnic cleansing and (although not overtly violent) other equally damaging forms of bigotry, all born out of the certainty of being right. Even in times of peace, as well as the 'good news of the gospel', Christian division and denominationalism has been exported across the world. Even the spread of the Anglican Communion, one has to acknowledge, has often been directly associated with the spread of the British Empire. Where Christian mission has gone wrong in the past is where there has been a refusal to engage in any meaningful way with the endemic cultures and philosophies to which the Christian faith is being brought other than to shout 'I am right and you are wrong'.

Alternatively, one can see mission as helping to discover a God who is already in their midst, encouraging faith communities to dialogue with, rather than preach at, members of other faith communities. It can also be seen as Christian communities recognizing Christ as the 'logos' though whom the world was created, as already being present in all creation, putting a name to that which already is, rather than introducing the idea that God is in some way absent from a group's cultural and personal experiences. Through the courtesy of listening to one another's stories, of listening to one another's songs, both personal and tribal, mission is then understood as being built on enabling, loving, respectful relationships, gently offering a spiritual viewpoint for consideration, always allowing for the fact that one might be wrong.

Who or what is mission for?

Is the primary point of mission to perpetuate an organization? Is it about increasing the quantity of its adherents? One can see mission purely in terms of numbers if one focuses on the fact that the Church as an organization will simply cease to function unless more people can be attracted to its ranks. In terms of the Church of England, it desperately needs more people to pay the parish share, more people to pay for stipendiary clergy. When more people are encouraged to join, then the more successful can the whole enterprise be seen to be.

Alternatively, one can see the primary point of mission as being about setting an individual free to live the life that God intends for a person to live in all its fullness, and deepening the quality of understanding of the message that lies behind this experience through continued nurture. Because it is in essence an outworking of the love of God incarnated in the world, the function of mission can be best understood as communication. Mission is the means whereby this love is proclaimed through word and in action in such a way that it is not experienced as being motivated by empire building or by the fear of extinction, but by the sure knowledge of being loved unconditionally always. Because this gift is freely received, it must be freely shared.

How does mission work?

Is it about knowing your product, knowing your audience, evolving strategies to sell the former to the latter, the whole being underpinned by a mission statement? Is it about targets and the pressure that comes with this? Is it about telling rather than listening? Is it about certainty rather than doubt? Is it about power rather than weakness? Is it about resurrection rather than crucifixion? Is it about engagement with a plan of action rather than disengagement with people's lived experience? Are mission statements about endings rather beginnings, summaries of what has been rather than strategies of what lies ahead? Because mission statements are so loved by business, there must be a real worry that they can be used as a kind of Trojan horse for secular values when reclaimed by faith communities from which they clearly sprang.

Alternatively, one can understand mission as working by responding to the needs of individuals who live in parishes, or come into contact with chaplaincies in their various forms, who are attracted to the Christian gospel, not through snappy teaching sound bites, not through razzmatazz events, but through their relationship with individual Christian men and women and the degree to which they sense God shining out of their lives, and are encouraged to think that God might be present in their own lives also, and are drawn to want to know more of the God who loves them unconditionally. When this happens, the language of success seems singularly inappropriate. More suited perhaps is the language of rejoicing, such as that experienced by the father in Jesus' parable of the Prodigal Son (Luke 15.1–30). Indeed, one can see mission at work by looking at Jesus' own ministry. It would seem to oscillate between the twin poles of 'come and see' and 'go out and tell'. When Jesus is newly born, people have to 'come and see', before they can 'go out and tell' what they have seen. Jesus' adult ministry starts with baptism and prayer before his active ministry takes off. When people want to know about Jesus' teaching and the kind of person that he is, he invites them to 'come and see'. In the case of his own disciples, once they have 'seen', then they are 'sent'. As the Church seeks to replicate this pattern, mission 'out there' must be underpinned by mission 'in here'. Mission 'out there' can be in danger of replicating a door-to-door sales person, communicating a prepacked vision of God. Because God is already there, a far better model to emulate is that of an archaeologist, discovering God afresh in and for each successive generation.

Mission Shaped Church: How is mission understood, who or what is it for, how does it work?

In his forward to the seminal document *Mission Shaped Church*, former Archbishop Rowan Williams says:

> If 'church' is what happens when people encounter the Risen Jesus and commit themselves to sustaining and deepening that encounter with each other, there is plenty of theological room for diversity of rhythm and style, so long as we have ways of identifying the same living Christ at the heart of every expression of Christian life in common. (Williams in Cray 2009, p.v)

Bishop Graham Cray, in his preface to the second edition of this document, is able to say that:

> Fresh Expressions…has become a movement involving all churchmanships and a wide range of age groups and social settings, a veritable 'mixed economy of ministry models'. (Cray 2009, p.vii)

Both these quotes appear to bode well for, and might seem to encourage, an inclusivity of parochial and non-parochial models of ministry. But further investigation reveals that there is no mention whatsoever of sector ministry, no mention of community and traditional models of chaplaincy and therefore no mention of pastoral care which is intrinsic to these particular ministries. Perhaps mission-shaped church is not to be so inclusive after all? And now, not surprisingly perhaps, one begins to glean the real thrust of mission-shaped imaginings: 'The long term value of any expression of Church, inherited or fresh, is to be judged by the sort of disciples its makes' (p.ix). 'Incarnational mission' (p.ix) seems to have no room for incarnational embodiment (after Whipp 2013, p.106). Is there to be no role for pastoral care in this brave new world of 'mission entrepreneurs' (Cray 2009, p.147)?

In its recommendations, at first glance, there appears to be some hope.

Recommendation 4, bullet point 2 states: 'Inherited ways of church and proposed fresh expressions of church need to work together in ways that are complementary to each other.' That surely must include chaplaincy.

Recommendation 9, in its reference to ecumenical working, talks of the importance of 'local…experiments and partnerships between Christians of different denominations'. Chaplains have been doing this for years.

Recommendation 10 talks not of cross cultural cooperation (of which many chaplains have a vast experience), but of 'cross cultural evangelism, church planting and fresh expressions of church' (pp.146, 147). Multi-faith working is not mentioned at all.

Despite drawing attention to the dangers of syncretism, this report 'in the attempt to be "relevant"' seems to have fallen into this danger itself (p.91), portraying pioneer ministers as trouble shooters, and mission as a consumerist activity.

Martyn Percy has looked at this from another perspective, wondering whether the Church is in danger of morphing from an institution into an organization. Whereas 'institutions…exist to propagate their values from one generation to the next', 'organizations are bodies that are free to adapt their focus in order to flourish' (2013). If the Church is regarded as an institution, 'what it cannot do is to try to change its focus. It risks losing its identity if it does' (2013). Percy compares this love affair that some in the Church have with numerical growth with the 'heresies and heterodoxies' of old. Like them, the lure of this present perceived panacea lies is in its simplicity (Percy 2014a). For the Church, the 'primary defining identity is the Body of Christ' (Percy 2013). Whereas organizations in general are productivity-driven, with growth in productivity being regarded as an indicator of its success, the Church in particular is about nurturing 'wisdom' and 'faithfulness', where value cannot simply measured in the number of people attending but in the enduring and sustaining quality of their faith. Whereas organizations have a management structure at their core, the Church's ministers can appear more like 'poets, artists or philanthropists', interpreting and living the reality of God's presence in the world 'occupied with God and…preoccupied with God's concerns' rather than just doing a job that is measurable and quantifiable (Percy 2013).

In his response to the Green Report (which looks at the selection and training of senior church leaders; Green 2014), Percy's worst fears seem to have been realized when organizational management styles have so infected ministerial formation.

> A small 'talent pool' of potential future leaders…will be selected and shaped by a handful of executive managers, and their selection and training facilitated by them. The criteria for joining the talent pool are controlled by these executive managers, who, in turn have determined the vocation of the Church, its strategic priorities, its goals and, to some extent, its identity. (Percy 2014b)

Percy notes that there is no mention of how this business model of leadership will engage 'with the primary calling of bishops…if bishops now move from being chief pastors to chief executives' (Percy 2014b).

If the Church moves more towards an organizational rather than an institutional structure, two areas of ministry that Percy sees as suffering are the Church's prophetic and pastoral ministry. Paradoxically, he sees this as adversely affecting its mission voice. The Church does not exist to grow exponentially. Mission is deeper than that. The Church exists to embody the command of Jesus to 'love the Lord with all our heart, mind, soul and strength, and our neighbours as ourselves' (Percy 2014a). As members of Christ's body, the Church, we do this in whichever context God has placed us. Understanding that context is key. It is not breadth but depth that is significant here. 'The Kingdom is about small numbers and enriching quality' (Percy 2014a). At its heart mission is not activity-driven but is relational.

My own diocese of Winchester (which in its mission strategy has set itself the task of 'becoming a mission shaped diocese' by 'living the mission of Jesus') has set itself four strategic priorities: 'growing authentic disciples; re-imagining the Church; enabling social transformation; and belonging together in Christ'. These are undergirded by 'the three Ps: passionate personal spirituality, pioneering faith communities and prophetic global citizenship'. Interestingly, there is no mention of pastoral care at all, not even passionate, personal, pioneering and prophetic pastoral care! Despite 'belonging together in Christ', neither is there any reference to sector ministry (Diocese of Winchester 2012). However, in a subsequent Lent course it is able to affirm that 'there is no divide between the pastoral and the missional. The Church's life together and its witness to the world is inseparable' (Diocese of Winchester 2016, p.41), suggesting that 'surely there must be another way of understanding a mission shaped church?'

Mission Shaped Church incorporating the provision of pastoral care: How is mission understood, who or what is it for, how does it work?

Practical theology and missiology

As a precursor to exploring the relationship of pastoral care to mission, it seems timely to briefly explore the relationship of practical theology to missiology. BIAPT (the British and Irish Association of Practical Theology) and BIAMS (the British and Irish Association of Missiology Studies) have key roles to play here. Having recently merged, they are actively exploring the relationship between practical theology and missiology. In an article which looked ahead to this 'merger' getting under way, Nigel Rooms and Cathy Ross explore what they consider to be the likely pros and the cons of this process. They observe that both are contextual; both address questions concerning meaning and identity of individuals and the communities in which they are set; both are interdisciplinary (in that they 'draw on…social sciences and anthropologies') and both are concerned with how faith is communicated to a wider culture (2014, p.145).

It is not surprising that they see a parallel between Graham, Walton and Ward's 'seven 'methods' of theological reflection' (i.e. 'Theology by Heart, Speaking in Parables, Telling God's Story, Writing the Body of Christ, Speaking of God in Public. Theology-in-Action, Theology in the Vernacular'; 2005, pp.13–14); and Bevan's 'five 'models' of contextual theology' (i.e. 'The Translation, Anthropological, Praxis, Synthetic and Transcendental Models'; 2002, pp.27–8). The differences that these two disciplines exhibit between them have to do with their origins and their respective contexts. 'Practical theology…

has emerged to some extent from the therapeutic world of counselling and psychotherapy, whereas missiology draws heavily from the field of Church history' (Rooms and Ross 2014, p.145). Their context is seen in the case of practical theology as being primarily local, whereas for missiology it is global. Both disciplines carry negative overtones from the past. Practical theology can be seen as allowing secular disciplines to over-influence the tradition of faith. Missiology can still 'be tainted by the colonialism of the Victorian missionary era' (p.146). For this merger to work, Rooms and Ross believe that practical theology must recover its global context and missiology recover its local context, God at work in the macro- and micro-dimensions of life.

Understanding pastoral care afresh in a mission-focused environment

It is essential for the Church both to understand pastoral care afresh in relation to mission, and to understand mission afresh in relation to pastoral care. For when the Church is in 'mission mode', Pattison believes (reflecting Percy's comments above), there seems to be a preference for nurturing:

> communication, management, organizational and leadership skills, not the skills of pastoral care and the essentially reflective attitudes that might be thought to accompany them. Furthermore, the pastoral dimension has been returned to the personal, the private, the passive and the introverted, and the individually pathological. (2008, p.8)

In other words, those very aspects of pastoral counselling, out of which the need for the separate discipline of pastoral care sprang. This viewpoint, within the context of the pastoral care exercised by hospital chaplains, would seem to be underlined by the Church of England bishop speaking on healthcare matters, James Newcombe (Bishop of Carlisle), who was reported as saying in an article that purported to articulate the importance of healthcare chaplaincy, 'It is very important to stress that chaplains are therapeutic, not evangelistic' (Drake 2015, p.22). Even if there seems to be a confusion here between pastoral counsellors and pastoral carers, there seems to be no sense whatsoever that chaplains are capable of enfleshing the love of God incarnationally, a rather strange state of affairs when all chaplains have to be authorized by their faith groups. In the light of Bishop Newcome's remarks, one cannot help but wonder why this faith-based authorization is necessary?

But can pastoral care in any way be considered as mission? In an article that considers whether academic research can be considered as mission (using a sentiment that is equally applicable pastoral care), Peter Gubi observes that as in research, so too '[i]n mission, one has to get alongside those with whom you are working and learn their language in order to communicate truth' (2012, p.59). Effective pastoral care relies on one's ability to 'get alongside' a person, to inhabit the space and language that they are inhabiting in order to embody, witness to and communicate transformative gospel truth.

As a way of redefining pastoral care in a mission-led Church, Pattison maintains that 'there is absolutely no reason why the "pastoral" should be cast primarily in the mode of a political status quo affirming personal care in time of difficulty' (2008, p.9). In other words, he would appear to be suggesting that pastoral care must also be about challenging politically unjust situations as they impinge on individuals and communities and having something meaningful to say about God to people when things are going well. He continues:

> If pastoral care is cast as attending and nurturing to God's world, and all that is in it for God's sake, then this is a mode of understanding and acting that is essential if mission is not to be about a rather crude preoccupation with a certain type of conversion and colonization. (p.9)

For Pattison, 'theologically informed' and 'practically relevant' pastoral care 'is an essential part of God's mission to the world' (p.9).

Understanding chaplaincy afresh in a mission-focused environment

Starting from an understanding of mission which 'is no longer seen as an optional activity undertaken by a particular kind of church, but rather the Church's core identity', Victoria Slater defines this identity as constituting 'the bearing of God's mission in the world', 'the "missio Dei"' (2012, pp.316, 317), which has echoes of Pattison's concept of pastoral care as 'attending and nurturing to God's world, and all that is in it for God's sake' (2008, p.9). Because she believes that each community in which this activity is to be undertaken must 'discern the shape of God's mission for each place and time' (Heywood 2011, p.113, cited in Slater 2012, p.316), a chaplaincy view of mission in which the chaplain is 'incarnating the goodness of God's love for the sake of the world' is as likely to be 'as relevant as any other' (p.317). As a way of countering the Church's thinking about mission that makes no significant reference to pastoral care in general, and sector ministry and chaplains in particular, Slater points out that for those 'who are closed to institutional belonging, but open to "God" in the transcendent,...chaplaincy (especially community chaplaincy) is one structure through which the Church is able to find ways of connecting with people' and 'taking account of personal experience' (p.313). This is made easier because, although this ministry works 'outside church structures', chaplains 'are embedded in social structures', those same structures as the people they are seeking to come alongside (p.313).

Furthermore, in chaplaincy, because it is primarily relational (because 'God is relational'; pp.69, 21), the agenda is not set by the wider Church's preoccupation by the need to make institutional disciples, but 'by the circumstances of the person with whom the chaplain is involved' (p.315). By the chaplain's presence, their manner, and in what they say or do not say, they seek to 'bring God into people's lives at a time when they are vulnerable without ramming it down their throats' (p.315). The theology may remain 'implicit' rather than 'explicit', but it is present none the less. She describes this as modelling 'an operant theology of mission' which being 'incarnated in practice understands service and pastoral care as being core dimensions of the Church's vocation to serve God's mission in the world' (pp.69, 71). This in no way precludes Pattison's point above of pastoral care necessarily also being about challenging politically unjust situations as they impinge on individuals and communities, and having something meaningful to say about God to people when things are going well. I have had experience of both of these points in my own healthcare chaplaincy ministry.

When a reconfiguration of learning disability provision took place which involved moving funding from communities to individuals and resulted in the closing of some day centres, I found myself being used as a shoulder to cry on by clients who could not understand why their day centre should close and why they would no longer be able to see their friends there. This managerial decision caused great anger amongst the staff who were feeling the pain of their clients. My role was to reflect this incomprehension and anger back to the managers and challenge their decision.

I remember visiting one terminally ill patient at the hospice at wintertime when snow had fallen during the night and was continuing to fall. The patient was an artist, and when I entered the room, she was in the process of sketching a snowflake which was hanging on a branch outside her window. She beckoned me over and wanted me to wonder with her at the beauty and the fragility of creation. I was not required to say anything other than to share in her joy.

Slater is clear that 'the bearing of God's mission in the world', both in times of sadness and of joy, can be costly to the chaplain as they 'need to be able to work in faith and trust with an element of not knowing' (2012, pp.316, 315). Chaplaincy is not a new pioneering ministry that needs to be invented. It's a pioneering ministry that exists already!

Conclusion

In order to prevent a perceived gulf between pastoral care and mission becoming ever wider and deeper, this chapter has argued that it is essential for the Church both to understand pastoral care afresh in relation to mission and to understand mission afresh in relation to pastoral care. There has been an acknowledgement that, in the past, pastoral care has suffered from being too exclusively clerical rather than incorporating all relevant authorized ministers, too problem-centred rather than growth-centred, too individualistic rather than communal, and in danger of ruling out pastoral need that didn't have its origins in the context of ultimate meanings and concerns (Pattison 1988, p.13). Furthermore, despite recognizing the uniqueness of each person's spiritual journey, pastoral care has run the risk of falling into therapeutic drift when it has failed to remain rooted within a community of faith, and of becoming too passive when it has failed to take 'seriously the social and political context of care 'by adjusting to injustice, rather than challenging and transforming (unjust) social structures (Lyall 2001, p.12). There has also been an acknowledgement that mission has suffered from prioritizing organizations over institutions, managers over pastors, quantity over quality, power over powerlessness, received tradition over lived experience, arrogance over humility, certainty over doubt, colonization over liberation, sound bites over informed dialogue, and of becoming too passive when it has failed to engage in any meaningful way with the cultural contexts in which it is working

In an article in which she portrays pastoral theology as paying attention to the voices of the pastoral encounter, theological tradition and the mission of the Church, Jane Leach seems to be saying the same thing. She also understands pastoral care afresh in relation to mission, by acknowledging that 'although I may be called to make a (pastoral) response in this time and place...my response needs to belong within the Church's understanding of mission' (2007, p.29). She also understands mission afresh in relation to pastoral care by underlining '[t]he need for us to practice spiritual attention...(when finding)...new ways of being church which are both responsive to God and our cultural context' (p.30). Only then, one feels, will the wider Church be able to acknowledge, both in times of sorrow and of joy, that pastoral relationships can give 'an embodied witness to the loving presence of God in the midst of ordinary human life' (Whipp 2013, p.106). Only then has pastoral care the potential to offer an integrated holistic pastoral performance.

> The song was sung and the song was heard...
> But as roots went down, it carried on floating,
> And new songs emerged, and new songs were sung.
>
> (Clifton-Smith 2016)

Conclusion

PASTORAL CARE AS 'MISSION PRAISE'

At the heart of this book has been the process of engaging in 'critical dialogue between theological norms', supported by historical examples of literal and metaphorical imprisonment; traditional 'norms' taken from healthcare literature (which range from the psychological through the clinical to the philosophical and theological); and reflecting upon whether these offer any illumination to the 'contemporary experience', particularly as they relate to the seven case studies of hospitalization (encompassing end-of-life care, bereavement, loss (suffered by individuals and groups)).

This process has been assisted by looking at pastoral care through the prism of classical music and to use this prism as a catalyst by way of presenting pastoral care in a new way. The use of this 'interdisciplinary approach' has shown how musical composition can, through the process of collage, dialogue tradition with experience; musical participation can provide a model for pastoral caring; and musical interpretation can provide a model for pastoral discernment. By comparing the five musical compositions born out of experiences of war and social fragmentation, with the experience of hospitalization; and the elements of contrasting musical polarities and musical form with the seven case studies in particular; the various musical functions of conductor, concert hall/chamber music salon, audience and of co-performer with that of the chaplain (pastoral carer); in thus reflecting the illumination that each discipline can bring upon the other, by representing the performative meaning-making cycle as embracing both the hermeneutic and pastoral cycles, I have suggested that music can indeed provide a meaningful language through which people can communicate the presence or absence of God through a process of 'theoretical and practical transformation' of the pastoral care encounter.

Finally, just as music has been used as a paradigm for how the past can relate to the present, so it is used as a model of how the future (mission-focused ministry of the Church) can relate to its ever-present ministry of pastoral care. Without being in relationship with each other, mission runs the risk of being a melody without harmony (imposing a tradition of faith upon contemporary experience), and pastoral care a harmony without melody (imposing contemporary experience upon a tradition of faith). When both are in complementary partnership and in vibrant relationship one with the other, they have the potential to enflesh the living God, in that song beyond words.

APPENDIX 1

ST JOHN OF THE CROSS – DARK NIGHT OF THE SOUL – PROLOGUE PP. 1–2 STANZAS OF THE SOUL

On a dark night,
Kindled in love with yearnings
– oh happy chance! –
I went forth without being observed,
 My house being now at rest.

In darkness and secure,
By the secret ladder, disguised
– oh happy chance!
In darkness and concealment,
My house being now at rest.

In the happy night,
In secret, when none saw me,
Nor beheld I aught,
Without light or guide,
Save that which burned in my heart.

This light guided me.
More surely than the night of noonday
To the place where he
(well I knew who!) was waiting me
– A place where none appeared.

Oh, night that guided me,
Oh, night more lovely than the dawn.
Oh, night that joined
Beloved with lover.
Lover transformed in the Beloved!

Upon my flowery breast,
Kept wholly for himself alone,
There he stayed sleeping,
and I caressed him.
And the fanning of the cedars made a breeze.

The breeze blew from the turret.
As I parted his locks:
With his gentle hand
he wounded my neck.
And caused all my senses to be suspended.

I remained lost in oblivion;
My face reclined on the Beloved.
All ceased and I abandoned myself,
Leaving my cares
forgotten among the lilies.

APPENDIX 2

TEXTS AND MUSICAL QUOTATIONS USED IN *COLLAGE*

Texts

1. The Collect for Purity & The Prayer of Humble Access from the Book of Common Prayer (1662)

2. 1 Corinthians 13 [AV]

3. The 'Tomorrow and tomorrow and tomorrow' speech from Shakespeare's *Macbeth*, Act V Scene V.

4. An account of drug withdrawal by Peter Laurie

5. Laurie, P. (1967) *Drugs – Medical, Psychological, and Social Facts.* Harmondsworth Penguin Books, pp.21, 23–4.

6. Matthew 26.39 [AV]

7. John 16.33 [AV]

Texts and musical examples

1. Setting of the words of the Creed

2. Setting of the words of the Gloria

3. Merbecke, J. (1568) *Office of Holy Communion.* G.H Knight (ed.) London: RSCM and SPCK.

4. Stanford, C.V. Psalm 150. *English Hymnal* No. 390.

5. Tune: London New C.M. (Music from the *Scottish Psalter* (1635) adapted by John Playford); Text: Cowper, W. 'God moves in a mysterious way.' *Hymns Old and New (Anglican Edition)* No. 173.

MUSICAL FORMS

Monothematic forms

(Where there is one main theme in evidence.)

Fantasia: A freely flowing musical form which, although written down, gives the impression of improvisation. It is often placed before, and in contrast with, a fugue.

Theme and Variations: As its name suggests, this form begins with a statement of the theme on which the whole of the piece is based, each subsequent variation being an embellishment of the original theme. Variation can be achieved by filling in or drawing out the melody or rhythm, changing the harmony, the key or the time signature. Often the movement will end by a restating of the original theme.

Cantus Firmus: This quotes a known theme (such as a hymn tune) often in longer notes than usual, against which other parts are constantly changing.

Ground Bass or Passacaglia: This is a form of Theme and Variations in which the same repeated theme occurs initially in the bass part (but subsequently can occur in any part) and where variety is achieved through the constantly changing other parts).

Fugue: This is the apotheosis of monothematic forms in which a theme is stated, then stated again coming in five notes higher, then stated again at the octave, then stated again at various intervals. Once the theme has been stated, it then needs to harmonize with the next statement of the theme, so the music builds up in a kind of lattice work structure. Because the fugal passages can be quite intense, these are punctuated by other musical passages known as episodes picking up on a rhythmic and melodic figures that have occurred before and developing it before the fugal subject is stated again.

Dualistic forms

(Where there are two or more themes in dialogue with each other. In that which follows, different letters of the alphabet represent different themes.)

Strophic (AB) Form: The simplest example where more than one musical idea is used is the strophic form of verse and chorus. Whereas each verse may have the same music but different words, and each chorus will have the same words and music, coupled with the fact that the verse of a song is often sung by a soloist or solo group whilst the chorus is likely to be joined in by all present, there is added contrast established between the two sections. Both sections are essential to the whole song but remain distinct. There is no interplay between them.

Da Capo (ABA) Form: All that is necessary to convert a strophic song into ABA is for it to begin and end with its chorus. (This raises the very important question concerning whether it is ever possible to truly repeat anything at all. The last chorus, although it may sound the same as the first chorus, feels different because of the experience of having been stated before (so it is not new to the ear), and because of hearing it in relation to the different material of the verse.)

Rondo (ABACADetc.A) Form: This form is a further development of the AB and ABA forms in which each 'verse' has different music, the unifying factor being the recurrent A material with which it must begin and end. A refining of Rondo form is the Bridge Rondo in which the second half of the form is a mirror image of the first half (e.g. ABACABA).

Sonata Form: This is the apotheosis of dualistic forms. Just as fugal form reached its zenith when faith was at its strongest in that period immediately before the Enlightenment, so the Sonata Form grew out of the 'thesis, antithesis, synthesis' ideas of the Enlightenment. A sonata form movement owes its drive to the harmonic journey that takes place within it. Sonata Form can be divided into three sections: Exposition, Development and Recapitulation. In the Exposition section, two or more themes (A1B1etc.) are introduced in differing keys. These are then developed through their interplay one with another before being recapitulated in the same basis key (A1B2etc.). A refining of Sonata Form is the Bridge Sonata Form in which in the Recapitulation the second subject appears before the first (B2A1).

THE PARABLE OF THE SONG SMITH

At the beginning of time, divine thought took breath,
And sang and sang, 'it was so very good'.
The song took root in the singer of songs,
Who was so very smitten with this salvic song,
that this shaper of songs is continually singing it,
Modally, tonally, serially singing it.
Those who have ears let them hear.

The song was sung and the song was heard,
And sometime its melody sunk to the earth.
It sank and it sank, but 'though it took root,
(Remembering interiors, forgetting exteriors),
In unpacking dreams and unpacking memories
floated no more and suffered and died.
Those who have ears let them hear.

The song was sung and the song was heard,
And sometime its melody floated and floated,
In Gregorian manner it gathered no moss,
Fauxbordons aside it gathered no dross,
And floated and flew to the ends of the earth,
It floated and flew without giving birth,
Those who have ears let them hear.

The song was sung and the song was heard,
And sometime its melody floated and floated,
And sometime its melody sank and sank.
But as roots went down, it carried on floating,
And new songs emerged, and new songs were sung.
Those who have ears to hear, let them hear,
Those have new songs to sing let them sing.
It's all so incredibly good.

(Clifton-Smith 2016)

BIBLIOGRAPHY

Barenboim, D. (2008) *The Guardian*, 13 December.

BCP (1970) *The Book of Common Prayer*. Oxford: Oxford University Press.

Begbie, J. (2000) *Theology, Music and Time*. Cambridge: Cambridge University Press.

Bevan, S.B. (2002) *Models of Contextual Theology* (revised and expanded edition). Maryknoll, NY: Orbis.

Bonhoeffer, D. (1971) *Letters and Papers from Prison* (abridged). London: SCM Press.

Bowen, M. (1982) *Michael Tippett*. London: Robson Books.

Bowen, M. (ed.) (1980) *Music of the Angels: Essays and Sketchbooks of Michael Tippett*. London: Eulenberg.

Boyce-Tillman, J. (2000) *Constructing Musical Healing: The Wounds that Sing*. London: Jessica Kingsley Publishers.

Boyce-Tillman, J. (2009) *Space for Peace*. Unpublished.

Boyce-Tillman, J. (2011) *Space for Peace* programme notes, 27 January, Winchester Cathedral. Unpublished.

Bryden, C. (2005) *Dancing with Dementia*. London: Jessica Kingsley Publishers.

Britten, B. (1997) *War Requiem*. London: Boosey and Hawkes Music Publishers. (Original work published 1962.)

Bulgakov, S. (1937) *The Wisdom of God: A Brief Summary of Sophiology*. London: Williams and Norgate.

Campbell, A. (1985) *Paid to Care*. London: Darton, Longman and Todd.

Carr, W. (1997) *The Handbook of Pastoral Studies*. London: SPCK.

Cassidy, S. (1988) *Sharing the Darkness*. London: Darton, Longman and Todd.

Clebsch, W.A. and Jaekle, C.R. (1975) *Pastoral Care in Historical Perspective*. New York, NY: Aronson.

Clifton-Smith, G. (1973 (revised 2010)) *Collage: In Memoriam Charles Ives*. Unpublished.

Clifton-Smith, G. (2013) *In the context of health care, where is God in the dark places of human experience? Implications for Pastoral Care*. DProf Thesis, University of Chester. Unpublished.

Clifton-Smith, G. (2016) *The Parable of the Song Smith*. Unpublished.

Clinebell, H. (1984) *Basic Types of Pastoral Care and Counselling: Resources for the Ministry of Healing and Growth*. London: SCM Press.

Cray, G. (2009) *Mission Shaped Church: Church Planting and Fresh Expressions in a Changing Context*, 2nd edition. London: Church House Publishing.

Diocese of Winchester (2012) *Becoming a Mission-Shaped Diocese*. Unpublished.

Diocese of Winchester (2016) *I Witness: Living the Mission of Jesus*. Unpublished.

Drake, G. (2015) 'Hospital chaplaincy under fire.' *Church Times*, 16 October.

Eiesland, N. (1994) *The Disabled God: Toward a Liberation Theology of Disability*. Nashville, TN: Abingdon Press.

Evans, P. (1979) *The Music of Benjamin Britten*. London: J.M. Dent and Sons.

Ford, D. (2007) *Christian Wisdom: Desiring God and Learning in Love*. Cambridge Studies in Christian Doctrine. Cambridge: Cambridge University Press.

Foskett, J. (1984) *Meaning in Madness: The Pastor and the Mentally Ill*. New Library of Pastoral Care. London: SPCK

Frank, A.W. (1997) *The Wounded Storyteller: Body, Illness and Ethics*. Chicago, IL: University of Chicago Press.

Frankl, V. (1974) *Man's Search for Meaning*. London: Hodder and Stoughton.

Fulkerson, M. (2007) *Places of Redemption: Theology for a Worldly Church*. Oxford: Oxford University Press.

Garrison, J. (1982) *The Darkness of God: Theology after Hiroshima*. London: SCM Press.

Gill, R. (2010) 'Public Theology and Music.' *International Journal of Public Theology* 4, pp.410–25.

Goldsmith, M. (1998) *Dementia, Ethics and the Glory of God*. Derby: Christian Council on Ageing.

Goldsmith, M. (2004) *In a Strange Land: People with Dementia and the Local Church*. Edinburgh: 4M Publications.

Golea, A. (1960) *Recontres avec Olivier Messiaen*. Paris: Juillard.

Graham, E., Walton, H. and Ward, F. (2005) *Theological Reflection: Methods*. London: SCM Press.

Green, L. (1990) *Let's Do Theology*. London: Mowbray.

Green, S. (2014) *The Green Report*. Available at www.churchofengland.org/media/2130591/report.pdf (accessed 23 April 2016).

Gubi, P. (2012) 'Engaging with Research as Mission.' *The Journal of Health Care Chaplaincy* 12:2, pp.59–65.

Heywood, D. (2011) *Reimagining Ministry*. London: SCM Press.

Hunsinger, G. (1991) *How to Read Karl Barth: The Shape of His Theology*. Oxford: Oxford University Press.

Hunter, V. (2004) *Desert Hearts and Healing Fountains: Gaining Pastoral Vocational Clarity*. St. Louis, MO: Chalice Press.

John of the Cross (2003) *Dark Night of the Soul*. Mineola, NY: Dover Publications.

John Paul II. (1999) *Letter of His Holiness Pope John Paul II to Artists*. Available at http://w2.vatican.va/content/john-paul-ii/en/letters/1999/documents/hf_jp-ii_let_23041999_artists.html (accessed 23 April 2016).

Kübler-Ross, E. (1970) *On Death and Dying*. London: Routledge.

Lake, F. (1966) *Clinical Theology*. London: Darton, Longman and Todd.

Leach, J. (2007) 'Pastoral Theology as Attention.' *Contact* 153, pp.19–32.

Lewis, A. (2001) *Between Cross and Resurrection: A Theology of Holy Saturday*. Grand Rapids, MI: Wm. B. Eerdmans Publishing Co.

Lyall, D. (1995) *Counselling in the Pastoral and Spiritual Context*. Buckingham: Open University Press.

Lyall, D, (2000) 'Pastoral Care as Performance' in S. Pattison and J. Woodward (eds) *The Blackwell Reader in Pastoral and Practical Theology*. Oxford: Blackwell Publishing.

Lyall, D. (2001) *Integrity of Pastoral Care*. London: SPCK.

MacMillan, J. (2008) 'In Harmony with Heaven.' *The Tablet*, 11 October, pp.12–13.

McDonald, S. (2003) *Memory's Tomb: Dementia and a Theology of Holy Saturday*. Derby: Methodist Homes for the Aged.

McFadyen, A. (2000) *Bound to Sin*. Cambridge: Cambridge University Press.

McFague, S. (1983) *Models of God in Religious Language*. London: SCM Press.

Matthew, I. (1995) *The Impact of God: Soundings from St John of the Cross*. London: Hodder and Stoughton.

Maurice, F.D. (1837) 'The Kingdom of Christ: or Hints on the Principles, Ordinances and Constitution of the Catholic Church' in *Letters to a member of the Society of Friends vol. 2*. London: J.M. Dent.

Mayne, M. (2006) *The Enduring Melody*. London: Darton, Longman and Todd.

Messiaen, O. (1941) *Quatuor pour la fin du temps*. Paris: Durand Editions Musicales.

Pailin, D. (1992) *A Gentle Touch*. London: SPCK.

Parkes, C.M. and Weiss, R.S. (1983) *Recovery from Bereavement*. New York, NY: Basic Books.

Parkes, C.M. (1996) *Bereavement: Studies of Grief in Adult Life*, 3rd edition. London: Routledge.

Pattison, S. (1988) *A Critique of Pastoral Care*. London: SCM Press.

Pattison, S. and Lynch, G. (2005) 'Pastoral and Practical Theology' in D. Ford (ed.) *The Modern Theologians*, 3rd edition. Oxford: Blackwell.

Pattison, S. (2007) 'Stuff Pastoral Theology.' *Contact* 154, pp.6–14.

Pattison, S. (2008) 'Is Pastoral Care Dead in a Mission-led Church?' *Practical Theology* 1:1, pp.7–10.

Percy, M. (2013) 'It's not an organisation: it's the Body of Christ.' *Church Times*, 22 November.

Percy, M. (2014a) 'It's not just about the numbers.' *Church Times*, 28 February.

Percy, M. (2014b) 'Are these the leaders that we really want?' *Church Times*, 12 December.

Pople, A. (1998) *Messiaen: Quator Pour La Fin Du Temps*. Cambridge: Cambridge University Press.

Rooms, N. and Ross. C. (2014) 'Practical Theology and Missiology – Can they live together?' *Practical Theology* 7:2, pp.144–7.

Slater, V. (2012) 'Living Church in the World: Chaplaincy and the Mission of the Church.' *Practical Theology* 5:3, pp.307–20.

Slater, V. (2015) *Chaplaincy Ministry and the Mission of the Church*. London: SCM Press.

Shapiro, E. and Carr, W. (1991) *Lost in Familiar Places: Creating New Connections between the Individual and Society*. London: Yale University Press.

Speck, P. (1978) *Loss and Grief in Medicine*. London: Balliere Tindall.

Stevenson-Moessner, J, (2008) *Prelude to Practical Theology: Variations on Theory and Practice*. Nashville, TN: Abingdon Press.

Stevenson, K. (2007) *Rooted in Detachment: Living the Transfiguration*. London: Darton, Longman and Todd.

Swinton, J. (2000) *Resurrecting the Person: Friendship and the Case of People with Mental Health Problems*. Nashville, TN: Abingdon Press.

Tippett, M. (1991) *Those Twentieth Century Blues: An Autobiography*. London: Hutchinson.

Tippett, M. (2007) *A Child of Our Time*. London: Eulenberg. (Original work published 1941.)

Vanier, J. (1989) *Community and Growth*, 2nd edition. London: Darton, Longman and Todd.

Vanier, J. (2004) *Drawn into the Mystery of Jesus through the Gospel of John*. Toronto, ON: Novalis.

Volf, M. (1996) *Exclusion and Embrace*. Nashville, TN: Abingdon Press.

Wells, S (2015) *Thought for the Day*, 21 September, BBC Radio 4.

Whipp, M. (2013) *SCM Studyguide Pastoral Theology*. London: SCM Press.

Wiiliams, R. (1983) 'Imagery, Religion' in A. Richardson and J. Barden (eds) *A New Dictionary of Christian Theology*. London: SCM Press.

Williams, R. (1994) 'Keeping Time' in *Open to Judgement: Sermons and Addresses*. London: Darton, Longman and Todd.

Winkett, L. (2010) *Our Sound is Our Wound*. London: Continuum International Publishing Group.

Woodward, J. (2000) 'The Relevance of Michael Wilson's Chaplaincy Research for Healthcare Chaplains Today.' *Contact* 131:3, pp.16–22.

Young, F. (1990) *The Art of Performance*. London: Darton, Longman and Todd.

Young, F. (1991) *Face to Face: A Narrative Essay in the Theology of Suffering*. Edinburgh: T and T Clark.

SUBJECT INDEX

AUTHOR INDEX

Lightning Source UK Ltd.
Milton Keynes UK
UKOW06f130150616

276270UK00009B/150/P

9 781785 920363